Help Yourself
A Guide to Self-Change

Jerry A. Schmidt

RESEARCH PRESS

2612 NORTH MATTIS AVENUE
CHAMPAIGN, ILLINOIS 61820

This book is dedicated to five OK people—
My wife Karen
My sons Cory and Ryan
Dad
Mom

Contents

Acknowledgments   vii

Part 1   The basics of self-change   1
  1   What are you going to get out of this?   3
  2   What do you want to change?   9
  3   Becoming a self-watcher   21

Part 2   Strategies for self-change   39
  4   What triggers you to act?   41
  5   Increasing motivation with payoffs   49
  6   Self-contracting   61
  7   Relaxing yourself   71
  8   Talking to yourself   83
  9   Is it working?   97
 10   Getting what you need   105
 11   How do you feel about yourself?   115

Acknowledgments

The author wishes to acknowledge Elmer Sphon, Ed.D., and Vernon Williams, Ph.D., for providing early training in and enthusiasm for nontraditional modes of treatment. The editorial skills and feedback from Dr. Harry Moore and various counseling students at the University of Denver are also gratefully acknowledged.

Part 1 *The basics of self-change*

The first three chapters will teach you the basics of self-change. First we'll discuss the fact that in order to "grow" you must be motivated to change. You must also set your own goals and attach numbers to these goals in order to help you move off "dead center." You will be taught how to be a self-watcher and you'll probably have a good time doing it.

Once you have finished Part 1, you will be ready to initiate a self-change program of your own. Part 2 will add more sophisticated techniques to the basics you've learned in Part 1 and will give you more alternative strategies to use in your growth process. So have at it! Help yourself!

What are you going to get out of this?

1

There are many psychiatric self-help books on the market. Most of them describe and analyze what is wrong with you, but few of them give you concrete strategies on how to change yourself. When you finished reading one of these self-help guides, you may have felt that you had some new insights about yourself. However, a week later you also may have felt that nothing in your life had really changed. The basic purpose of *Help Yourself* is to give you several specific strategies for self-change.

Some of the self-help books you read in the past may have really fired you up about changing or accepting yourself. They may have inspired you to try to change. It also is likely that the "philosophies of life" presented in these guidebooks have led you to some new beliefs about the way life should be lived. Yet you still persist in your old self-defeating ways.

Or perhaps you have left a therapy session or read a chapter in a psychology book feeling even more confused and upset than when you started. You may have spent many hours talking about and thinking about all of your problems and idiosyncratic behaviors. At that moment you may have felt that your mind was bursting with ideas and insights that you were frantically trying to put together. All you knew was that something was wrong and that the book said, "Go see a psychologist" or that your therapist said, "This will take time to sort out." I agree with the therapist; it does take time. But when you are confused about "where your head is at," statements, such as, "This will take time," may not be very helpful.

This book is designed to help you "sort out" some of your difficulties and teach you to be a "self-changer." It can be used as a supplement to psychotherapy, or on your own, as a guidebook to better mental health.

I have attempted to supply you with a manual of step-by-step actions that you can engage in to bring about tangible changes in your life. I have tried to make these strategies so well defined that reading about them will lead to direct action. In other words, after having defined what is wrong, you will be guided, step by step, toward possible solutions. It may also be that you will decide that nothing is wrong and that all you really need are some strategies for accepting yourself more fully. Several chapters in this book deal with tactics for acceptance of self.

Motivation
As you read the preceding paragraphs, you may have thought about a few things you would like to change in your own life. Perhaps you are overweight and wish to reduce. Or possibly you have been told by your doctor to cut down on certain foods because of an ulcer, yet you continue to drink lots of cola or coffee. It could be that you wish to listen more carefully to what your spouse has to say at the end of a day, yet you find yourself forgetting to try.

In order to receive maximum benefit from *Help Yourself* you must already want to change what you don't like. The words *self-control* mean that *you* are the manager of treatment and change; you will be in charge of your own treatment program. The following chapters will be less inspirational and perhaps more instructive and technique-oriented than other self-help books. Although I will occasionally prod and urge you to take action, the primary purpose here is not to increase your motivation. The primary purpose is, rather, to give you specific ways to utilize that motivation in practical ways. If motivation is to become useful, it must be channeled toward productive action. But you will have to supply much of the initial motivation. The intervention strategies discussed throughout this book hopefully will inspire you to continue the process of becoming a better person.

I do not promise instant success. The field of psychotherapy and counseling is not developed to the point where we can prescribe various treatments for this and that problem. However, in my own practice as a therapist I have found that the procedures described throughout this book have been quite successful, and an increasing amount of research evidence indicates that these methods are effective.

How to Use This Book

Begin with Chapters 2 through 6; then read Chapter 9. If the methods discussed in these chapters do not work, suggestions will be made for reading one or more of the remaining chapters. Chapters 3, 7, 8, 10, and 11 can each be used independently for individual self-change programs. On the other hand, you may want to read the entire book before beginning your self-change plan. That is okay also. However, you should not skip to other chapters without first reading at least Chapters 1-3.

Beginning Your Own Self-Change

Take some time now to interview yourself. Take stock of what you want to do with your life. What goals do you have or what goals would you like to have? Are you satisfied with your career? Do you like what goes on between you and members of your family? Do you wonder sometimes why certain people really get your goat or why others seem to avoid you? To get the answers to some of these questions and other similar questions, try the following exercise.

Self-Interview Exercise

Write a short paragraph answer to the following questions.

1. What are five activities that you would like to be doing five years from now?
2. If you had a million dollars tax free, what would you do with it?
3. If you were a Martian and had two weeks to spend on planet earth, what would you do during those two weeks? Account for your time.
4. What makes you feel good?
5. Are there things about your family life that you would like to improve? If so, what are they?
6. If there was one thing you could change about yourself, what would it be?
7. What would you like to do more of in order to "get away from it all"?
8. What are you most afraid of?

The answers to this exercise will help you identify some areas of self-improvement. It may show you how far from your life goals you presently are. On the other hand, it also may show you how well you are meeting your own goals.

In any case this exercise is a good way to start "pinpointing" what you want to change, the subject of Chapter 2. Have fun with it! Allow yourself some time to play with it. Exercise your ability to fantasize. Don't throw it away. You will need it in the next chapter.

What do you want to change? 2

Now that you have finished the self-interview exercise in Chapter 1, you undoubtedly have several goals in mind. Some of them may be rather surprising. At this point, however, they are probably rather abstract and nebulous. For example, you might have answered question six by saying, "I want to lose weight," or "I want to enjoy my job more." Other possible goals include:

I want to stop smoking.
I want to spend more time studying.
I wish to spend less time being depressed.
I would like to fight less with my spouse.
I would like to be able to speak up in a group.
I would like to be more at ease with other people.
I would like to be more attractive to the opposite sex.
I want to stop nail-biting.
I would like to spend more time writing.
I would like to be more pleasant toward my parents.
I need more time for myself.
I would like to be able to express my opinion more often.

These statements certainly are beginning steps toward self-change, but they still do not tell you what to do. The purpose of this chapter is to teach you how to move from general goals like those above toward *action* programs through a process called *pinpointing*.

Pinpointing

The goal "I want to stop smoking" can provide a good example of pinpointing. This is clearly a noble goal for any smoker to set. If you set such a goal for yourself, it means that you must *stop* smoking *all* cigarettes. This is the only way many smokers seem to be able to "kick the habit." However, many people find it impossible to stop smoking completely. For these persons a more reasonable goal might be to "cut down gradually" on the number of cigarettes they smoke per day.

For example, a young woman who was smoking two packs (forty cigarettes) per day set a goal of cutting back to twenty cigarettes per day. When she stabilized at around twenty, she set a second goal of fifteen per day, then ten per day, and finally was able to even out at an average of eight cigarettes per day during a month's time. This woman had decided to *pinpoint* her goals to make them easier to attain. She set goals with numbers attached to them: "I will smoke only twenty cigarettes per day."

When you set goals with numbers attached to them, the goals become clearer, more readily attainable, and you are better able to judge whether you have reached them or not. If the woman who was trying to quit smoking had stated her goal as, "I will cut down on smoking gradually," she probably would have accomplished little, if anything. Instead, she had specific goals to work toward, and she knew when she had achieved them.

Pinpointing, then, is setting goals with numbers attached to them so that you or someone else can watch what you do or think and thus actually measure your progress toward your goals. The smoker in our example could watch herself and count the number of cigarettes she smoked every day. Because numbers were attached to her goals, she could tell whether she was *cutting down gradually* or not. The goals were clear, and because she knew that she was cutting down, she was motivated to set new numerical goals that eventually helped her to move from two packs (forty cigarettes) to only eight cigarettes per day.

At this point you might ask, "Okay Mr. Wizard, what happens if she sets these nice little numerical goals and doesn't reach them; then what?" Then she might need to make the goals more attainable. For example, instead of jumping from two packs per day to only twenty cigarettes, she might want to reset the goal at thirty-five per day.

There is absolutely *nothing wrong* with setting small goals. They are more reachable and realistic than large ones anyway. Many people mistakenly believe that they must change drastically in order to be successful. And when they fail to reach these unrealistic goals, they become disillusioned with themselves because they have not changed overnight or because they have regressed to their usual behavior after a few days.

We regress because *we* expect too much change too quickly. It takes time and small steps to overcome those things we wish to change—just as it has taken time to become who we are. We can call this practice of setting small goals *making mole hills out of mountains.* Decreasing the number of cigarettes smoked from two packs per day to thirty-five cigarettes is a significant change. It should be celebrated. It is a mole hill worth noting!

Another good reason for pinpointing and developing

mole hills is that it gets you off dead center. You *do* something about your life goals. Weak, mountainous, global goals, such as, "I would like to stop smoking," or "I would like to spend less time being depressed," only serve to perpetuate our inertia. Research tends to indicate that an individual has a better chance of reaching goals (thus a better chance of changing) that are stated in specific terms.

Moving from the Mountains to the Mole Hills

This is a good time to change some foggy, large goals into smaller, more specific ones. For each of the general goals listed below, I have developed more specific goals. These "mole hills" represent small, specific acts that together help to accomplish the general goal. I have also left a few blank spaces so that you can add more "mole hills" to the list. Fill in as many of the blanks as you can. The practice will help you pinpoint what you want to change later.

Making Mole Hills out of Mountains

Mountain:
I want to spend more time studying.

Mole Hills:
1. I will study for two fifteen-minute periods per day.
2. I will study for thirty minutes in the morning before I allow myself to eat lunch.
3. I will read and outline one chapter in my history book each week day.
4. Today I will refuse one request that will take me from my studies (request made by a friend to play tennis or golf or to get something to eat).
5. (You add one) _____

6. (One more, please) _____

_____

_____

Mountain:
I wish to spend less time being depressed.

Mole Hills:
1. I will count the number of times I feel good today.
2. Each day I will write down all the "good" things that happen to me. My goal is to find at least two per day.
3. Each time I do something right I will spend five minutes becoming immersed in positive thoughts about it. My goal is to spend at least ten minutes per day engaged in positive thoughts.
4. If I am feeling depressed for more than thirty minutes, I will talk to a friend.
5. (You add one) _____

_____

_____

6. (Another one, please) _____

_____

_____

Mountain:
I wish to spend less time fighting with my spouse.

Mole Hills:

1. I will not allow myself to get into more than one fight per day. A fight lasts for more than five minutes and involves cussing, calling my spouse names, and bringing up the "dark" past to make a point.
2. I will cut my nagging from the present average of twenty to ten "nags" per day.
3. I will allow myself to criticize my wife only two times per day for the next three weeks.
4. (You add one) _____

_____

_____

5. (Another one, please) _____

_____

_____

6. (And another) _____

_____

_____

Mountain:
I would like to speak up more in a group.

Mole Hills:

1. Each time I am in a group, I will ask at least one question of the person I feel closest to in the group.
2. At least once during each of the next three group sessions (social problems class), I will say out loud "I agree" to a statement someone else makes.

3. I will express a personal opinion at least twice during the next neighborhood party.
4. I will average three statements per group meeting for the next two weeks.
5. (You add one) _____

_____

_____

6. (Another one, please) _____

_____

_____

Mountain:
I need more time for myself.

Mole Hills:
1. I will spend one hour per week playing tennis.
2. I will allow myself at least one evening of pleasure reading per week.
3. I will spend at least three dollars per week for a babysitter while I am involved in some activity, such as fishing, tennis, golf, or shopping for antiques.
4. I will ask my boss for at least one personal leave day per three-month working period.
5. I will plan at least three weekend outings to the mountains for this summer.
6. (You add one) _____

_____

_____

7. (Add another, please) _____

_____

_____

8. (And another) _____

_____

_____

If you are going to change, you first must want to change. Then you must identify some important goals. These goals should be very similar to the ones you discovered while doing the self-interview exercise in Chapter 1. Then, begin the action process by pinpointing your goals and breaking them down into smaller steps, or "mole hills," as you have just done in the above exercise.

What next? Next you might try to decide on the difficulty of your goals. For example, is cutting the number of "nags" from twenty to ten per day realistic? Would cutting them to fifteen per day be more realistic? There is one simple way to test your alternatives. Set what you think is a reasonable goal and then try to accomplish it. If you cannot reach that goal, your world won't come crashing down around you. Make the goal easier to reach. You could drop back, in this case, to fifteen nags per day during the first week of attempted change. During the second week you again could try ten. Or you could try an even slower rate by beginning the second week with a goal of twelve nags per day. The important thing is to break your goal down into small enough steps to maximize your chances for progress.

A second question related to the difficulty of goals must be answered. "How do you know how many times per day you have been nagging your spouse? How do you know it was twenty times?" The only way you can know the number of nags is to have someone count them for about a week and find the average number per day. The average number (in this case, twenty) tells you where to begin goal setting. You should begin somewhere under twenty.

You may have thought of another question: "What is a nag and what is not a nag?" Words or terms such as *nags, positive self-thoughts, arguments,* and *critical remarks* are subjective. Few people agree about exactly what they mean. If someone else counts your nags, you will know what at least one other person thinks nagging is. For example, you might ask your spouse to count nags. Your spouse can decide arbitrarily when a statement feels like a nag. "Refusing a request" may be defined as "refusing a request that a friend makes to play tennis, football, or golf, or to get something to eat." A marital fight could be defined as "a quarrel that lasts for more than five minutes and involves cussing, calling my spouse names, and bringing up the 'dark' past to make a point."

Your goals not only should be pinpointed and broken down into "mole hills," but they should also be as clearly defined as possible. That may not sound very exciting or inspirational, but you'll have a better chance for change if you do so. At this point go back to the exercises on making mole hills. Your goals should look very much like the "mole hills" listed there.

Your Own Self-Change: Step Two
Look again at your self-interview exercise in Chapter 1.

Make a check mark next to three of your answers that suggest important personal goals for you. From those three select the one answer that you think is the most exciting, yet attainable, goal. For example, to question eight (What are you most afraid of?), you might have answered, "I am most afraid of death and the idea that one day I will die."

You may have checked this answer because it suggests a very important personal goal: "I want to minimize my fear of death." In some cases you may have to rewrite your answer in order to develop it into a goal. You not only can do this—you should if it makes your goal clearer. (Many of the questions in the self-interview exercise were designed so that your answer would be a goal statement, such as, "If I could change one thing about myself it would be to lose some weight.")

When you have checked the goal you feel is perhaps most important for you, you have identified your *mountain.* You can break this mountain into mole hills by writing five goals that will help you attain the mountain. *Remember,* make sure that your mole hills have numbers attached to them, that they are realistic and attainable, and that they resemble the mole hills in the section of this chapter called "Making Mole Hills Out of Mountains."

You may want to sequence the mole hills so that the first goal must come before the second goal. For example, if your goal is to lose weight, your "mole hills" may look something like this:

1. During the first two weeks of self-change, I will reduce my weight from 145 pounds to 140 pounds.
2. During the third week of self-change, I will reduce to 138 pounds.
3. During the fourth week of self-change, I will reduce

my weight to 136 pounds.

By all means make the mole hills small and attainable! More noble intentions have been abandoned because people expected too much change too fast. If you can arrange the steps so that they must come in a certain order, do so. You may set up your five mole hills so that you work on one each week for five weeks. Or you may elect to work on all five for a couple of months. Do whatever seems to maximize your chances for success.

At this stage you have decided that you are motivated to change something about yourself, you have developed some general goals, and you have "pinpointed" them and made "mole hills" out of "mountains." You may be closer to self-change at this moment than you have been for some time. Now what? Follow me to Chapter 3.

Becoming a self-watcher 3

Self-Watching

I'm depressed. It seems that everything I do turns into a bummer. Sometimes I lie awake all night worrying about the next day. Other times I take an all afternoon nap just so I don't have to think or worry about the day. I'm just plain down all of the time.

When one of my young clients said this to me in her first therapy session, her situation sounded pretty hopeless. She had come to the conclusion that everything she came into contact with was depressing. After a bit of conversation it became rather obvious to both of us that she spent a good deal of time noticing events that were disagreeable to her. For example, whenever her husband did not kiss her good-bye in the morning, she would become immersed in negative thoughts about her marriage and how undesirable she must be to her husband. She could not recall any of her feelings or thoughts on those days when her husband left for work and did kiss her good-bye. It was as if she was looking for depression. That is, she frequently became absorbed in thoughts about negative events but seldom became preoccupied with positive ones. I asked Sally to notice and record on paper any event that was desirable to her for a one-week period. I did not ask her to change any of her thoughts or to do anything else differently except to look for the positive incidents. The table on the next page shows Sally's observations over a week's time.

When Sally began looking for positive things, she found them. Perhaps there are not as many good things going on in Sally's life as yours, but her "self-watching" brought seventeen happy times to Sally's attention. I then encouraged Sally to concentrate on some of these positive events. I asked her to take five minutes immediately after one positive happening each day to immerse herself in enjoyable thoughts and feelings concerning that happening. One week of self-watching helped to identify some therapeutic strategies that led Sally out of depression and away from a possible suicide attempt.

What Can Watching Yourself Do for You?

Knowing What to Change

Sometimes just watching yourself changes your behavior. For example, a bright thirty-year-old doctoral student at a large state university found himself worrying constantly about the outcome of a relationship with a girl friend. He became so obsessed with his problem that he could not concentrate on his studies, which only made things worse, because he also worried about whether he would make it through a rather rigorous graduate program or not. He told me, "I'm literally eating my heart out over a situation I have no control over anymore. She's leaving me anyway, but I can't get her out of my mind."

Tom decided to watch himself. With the help of a golf counter, which can be purchased at most sporting goods stores, he began counting the number of times he

Noticing Positive Events

Saturday	Sunday	Monday	Tuesday	Wednesday	Thursday	Friday
1. A friend called and asked me how I was feeling.	1. Harold and I looked at model homes.	1. Harold did kiss me good-bye.	1. Nothing good happened!	1. I planted some more rose bushes.	1. Harold kissed me good-bye.	1. Someone said that I looked good today.
2. Joanie (her daughter) said, "I love you Mommy."	2. Harold and I and the kids went to the mountains for a picnic.	2. I went out to lunch with a girl friend.		2. I was invited to a neighborhood coffee.	2. Felt good about only taking half-hour nap today.	
3. I got three ripe tomatoes out of our garden.		3. I began reading a new book, *I Ain't Much Baby But I'm All I've Got*.		3. I watched my favorite TV program.	3. Read a book to Peter (her son) this p.m.	
		4. Harold and I made love on the sofa.		4. I did not think about suicide today.		

23

thought about the girl each day. He divided the thoughts into two categories: short, if he just thought about her for a few seconds, and long, if he thought about her for a longer period of time (one to thirty minutes). Although the main purpose of watching himself was to pick up clues for possible ways to treat his problem, Tom discovered that just counting his "girl friend thoughts" was helpful. The effectiveness of Tom's "self-watching" is shown in the diagram below.

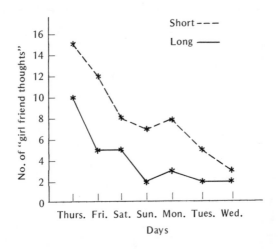

Tom spent three more weeks counting short and long thoughts. At the end of this time he reported that he was sleeping better, eating better, and having more fun on dates with other girls.

Putting Your Finger on the Trigger

You can discover what triggers (or causes) you to react the way you do. Jim, a thirty-five-year-old high school teacher, was concerned about his relationship with his four-year-old son, Cory. Jim found himself constantly criticizing his son.

Cory reacted to his father's faultfinding by running to his room, crying to his mother, and throwing a tantrum. To make things even worse Jim's wife continuously nagged him about his critical remarks.

Jim watched his negative interactions with his son for a week. He discovered several events that seemed to trigger his nasty comments:

1. He spilled milk on the table or on the floor.
2. He poured ketchup all over his food and on the table.
3. He dropped his cereal on the table.
4. He took all of his toys out of his toy box and spread them all over the house.
5. He used delaying tactics when he was supposed to be getting dressed for school in the morning or getting ready for bed at night.

Now Jim had a few handles on the events that caused him to make overly critical remarks. He developed several strategies. One, since Cory loved ketchup, Jim decided to provide an alternative method for his son to use it. At the beginning of each evening meal, Jim simply poured some ketchup in a small bowl and let Cory spread ketchup on his food with a spoon. This eliminated the "bloody" drama caused by the lake of ketchup on Cory's plate.

Jim used a second strategy to encourage Cory to pick up his toys. He placed small, attractive toy boxes in each room of the house. He thought that the mere sight of these colorful toy boxes would catch Cory's eye and jog his memory. He would be more likely to want to put his toys in these pretty "houses"—no matter what room he was in.

Jim used several other schemes to cut down on the number of situations that triggered his anger at Cory. In other chapters I will return to this case in order to illustrate other methods of self-control. At this point it is enough to say that by discovering what was triggering him to react negatively to Cory, Jim was able to make a noticeable difference in his relationship with his son and wife.

Payoffs

You can discover if there are any "payoffs" for your undesirable reactions. A payoff is a result or consequence, in other words, what you get from your actions. You can discover "payoffs" while you are watching yourself. (There is more about payoffs in Chapter 5.)

Ruth, a middle-aged woman, wished to improve her marriage by cutting down on the nagging answers she gave her husband. She was not fully convinced, however, that her nags were all that detrimental and destructive to their relationship. A week of self-watching produced several payoffs. Following a day of a high number of "nags," Ruth's husband would leave more clothes lying on the floor and chairs; there seemed to be a direct relationship between number of nags and the number of pieces of clothing and other articles lying around the house. She also noticed that, on those evenings when she nagged the most, they did not have sex. Since she was very concerned about their sex life, she began to realize her nagging might be the cause of an unwanted payoff: an unsatisfying sex life. This discovery led the couple to seek out a sexologist who in turn helped them improve not only their sexual relationship but also their marriage in general.

Is It Really That Bad?

You may discover that your "problem" is really not a "problem." Mr. and Ms. Gibson were concerned about their daughter Tammy, who they felt was too aggressive. They had taken a psychology class together and had learned about the "aggressive child." They were convinced that Tammy needed to see a child psychiatrist. When they asked me to refer them to someone for such help, I urged them first to try an experiment that would take only a few days. I asked them to describe Tammy's aggressive actions. These actions included pushing another child, shouting at another child, taking a toy away from another child, and breaking other children's toys.

The next step was to observe Tammy playing with other children for a few half-hour periods, counting the number of "aggressive" acts each child engaged in. We managed to enlist the help of a neighbor so that mother, father, and neighbor were each counting the same thing independently—aggressive acts as defined by the Gibsons. The findings suggested that Tammy was no more aggressive than the children she played with. In fact the neighbor's count showed Tammy to be the least aggressive of the four children. Tammy's mother and father counted more aggressive acts for Tammy than for two of the other children, but they also discovered that one of the children (also a girl) reacted aggressively *more often* than Tammy!

Further discussion revealed that Mary and Steve Gibson had come from families that regarded assertive or aggressive acts as unkind and sinful. We also discussed the notion that young children often have difficulty sharing toys and sometimes even break things that they like. Once the Gibsons actually observed Tammy, they were much more open to judging her behavior in relation to other children. Thus they would be less likely to label her in a negative fashion in the future.

You can use a similar method to evaluate your own behavior. You and a friend can observe your behavior independently and compare notes. What you think is a problem may not come through as a problem to someone else. But if you try this type of experiment, be sure to pinpoint what you're watching, as the Gibsons did. At this point you may want to review pinpointing in Chapter 2.

The Ties That Bind
You may discover behavior chains and thought chains. A man who consumed about a pint of vodka before going to bed each night for several months suddenly found that he could not go to sleep without it. During his self-watching program, he noted the following usual chain or sequence of events that led to drinking: coming home, turning on the TV, going to the refrigerator, putting ice in the glass, pouring the drink, going to the bathroom, undressing, showering, going to bed, and pouring more drinks.

The man rearranged this chain. He took a shower just after coming home, delayed going to the refrigerator until after undressing, and substituted cola for vodka in the glass. Although this type of strategy may sound somewhat simplistic, it has worked for a number of people. The vodka drinker, in this case, found himself consuming less alcohol because the chain of events that previously had led to maximum drinking had been broken up.

How to Be a Self-Watcher
As discussed in Chapter 2 your first step in a self-change project is to pinpoint what you want to change. Once you have decided this and can define the change you want to make in your behavior, thoughts, or feelings, it is time to ask the question, How will I count and watch what I am doing?

Counting Your Actions

There are at least three different methods used in self-watching: (1) watching events (counting total number of events); (2) watching the duration of an event; (3) time-sampling (counting the number of events that occur during specific time periods).

Sally, the depressed woman, and Ruth, the nagger, two of the women discussed earlier in this chapter, used the *watching events* method. Sally recorded every desirable event that happened to her during a week's time. In the same way Ruth counted every nag. If it is easy to count the total number of individual events, the watching events method can be very effective.

In some cases counting only the number of events may not be very helpful. Tom, the jilted young doctoral student, used a different method on his second self-change project. He wanted to decrease his telephone talking. At first he tried to count the number of phone calls he made per day, but he soon discovered that watching events was not a helpful tactic. On some days Tom would make only one call, but it would last for two or three hours. On other days he made several calls that lasted only a few minutes each. So, he switched to a second method of counting behavior—*watching the duration of an event*. That is, he began counting the total amount of time spent on the phone per day.

Choosing a method of counting is a matter of deciding what works. Since every situation is different, you will need to experiment. A middle-aged bachelor, who was extremely frightened of women, soon found that it was silly for him to count the amount of time he spent with females, because it totaled around four or five minutes a week. Instead he counted the number of occasions on which he said "hello" to an eligible woman and therefore had opportunity to spend time with her. Thus, he had begun counting using the *watching duration* technique but soon discovered that *watching events* was the proper method to use.

The Gibsons, the parents who were concerned about their daughter Tammy, needed a different approach. They used the time-sampling method of counting. They could not feasibly watch their daughter play all day for a week, so they observed her during one thirty-minute period each day. If time constraints keep you from watching yourself all day, use the time-sampling approach. That is, pick the same time or times each day and watch yourself *only* during those times. For example, a businessman and nightclub entertainer wished to cut down on his nail biting in public. However, it was nearly impossible to be consciously observing himself all day. Consequently, he chose to watch his nail biting from 11:30 a.m. to noon—when he experienced the most anxiety about his business—and from 8:30 p.m. to 9:00 p.m.— when he was anxious about his performance at the nightclub.

A young woman, Holly, decided that she wanted to eliminate a particular four-letter word from her vocabulary because she felt it was unnecessary and was "turning people off." She attempted to use the watching events technique of counting, but she found that she was using the word in almost every other sentence. Knowing the number of occurrences was not very helpful. So she decided that time sampling was a more practical method of counting.

What, then, should *you* be counting? If you have read

Chapter 2, you know how to pinpoint so that your behavior is tangible enough for you and/or others to recognize. Once you have pinpointed what you wish to change, you decide on a way to count behavior. The following rule ought to help you in making this decision: If the behavior, thought, or feeling occurs thirty or less times per day, and if it is easy to count the number of separate times the event occurs, use the watching events method. If the event occurs more than thirty times per day, use the time-sampling method. If the event is not easy to count or if it runs for several minutes at a time, employ the watching duration method—counting the amount of time the event takes.

Counting Accurately

A young man, Robert, wished to improve his listening skills. It seemed that almost every time someone spoke to him he would soon be preoccupied with other thoughts and eventually would say the telltale "huh?" and ask the speaker to repeat what he had said. Robert clearly communicated that he had not been listening. He made people rather angry because of this habit.

Since "huh" occurred well over thirty times per day, Robert decided to use the time-sampling method for counting. He thought about carrying around a notecard and making a check on it every time he said "huh" during his two fifteen-minute time samples. But he discovered that this was not practical. Instead, he counted by moving pennies from his left to his right front trouser pocket each time he noticed himself saying "huh." At the end of a fifteen-minute time sample Robert simply counted the pennies in his right pocket. Using pennies made the counting process much smoother, less obvious, and less distracting than the notecard technique.

Some self-watchers use golf counters to count. They can be purchased in most any sporting goods store and fit nicely in a pocket so that you can count secretly and still look cool (one hand in a pocket and one out). On the other hand, you may wish to advertise the fact that you are a "self-watcher" by wearing a wrist counter.* I do, and no one I have talked to has been offended.

A thirty-eight-year-old housewife and part-time student wanted to increase her vocabulary. Whenever she encountered a word she didn't know, she wrote it down, and later looked up its meaning in a dictionary. She was then able to count both the number of words written down and the number of words actually looked up. By increasing the percentage of words she looked up, she had an intelligent, convenient way to count and record her behavior.

Whatever you do, don't rely on your memory. Count your pinpointed events when they occur. If you try to remember the number of times something happens in order to write it down at the end of the day, your count will most likely be inaccurate and your self-control program will crumble. You can use golf-counters, wrist counters, or 3x5 notecards to help you count accurately. Or, you can devise your own techniques, such as transferring pennies from one pocket to another or tearing notches in a leaf.

Record Keeping: The Chart and the Graph
Once you have pinpointed and tinkered enough with

* Several companies sell wrist counters. Two of them are: H & H Enterprises, P.O. Box 3342, Lawrence, Kansas 66044; Behavior Research Company, Box 3351, Kansas City, Kansas 66103.

counting events to discover which counting method and what apparatus (pennies, a notecard, or a counter) to use, you must develop a permanent record-keeping system. That is, you must put your numbers into written form.

Sally wished to have a detailed record of "positive events," so she wrote them down on a chart (see p. 23). Tom was interested in recording the number of times he had "girl friend thoughts," but he was not interested in the details. His record-keeping system was a graph.

Charts generally are used for jotting down details of an event. These details often are useful in discovering what triggers your responses and also what payoffs may be forthcoming. Jim, the hypercritical father, discovered what was triggering his criticism of his son. He unearthed these insights by writing on a chart the details of each critical remark he made. Ruth, the "nagger," discovered certain undesirable payoffs by recording her behavior in the same manner. Charts will be discussed in more detail in Chapters 4 and 5.

A graph is less detailed than a chart. It is a pictorial summary of your behavior, thoughts, and feelings. The graph on the following page records the number of cups of coffee consumed each day.

The person who developed this graph was concerned about the number of cups of coffee she drank in a day. Her stomach was often upset, and she suspected that the amount of coffee she drank contributed to this. She became even more alarmed and motivated to change when she saw exactly how many cups she drank each day. Notice that the events she was counting (cups of coffee drank) are shown on the vertical portion of the graph and that the time units (days of the week) appear on the hori-

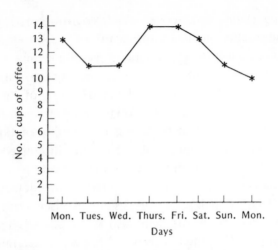

zontal. When you make a graph of your own events, you should organize the graph in the same way: events on the vertical; time units on the horizontal.

The Graph as a Motivational Tool

A rather reserved young lady wanted to become more conversational, more outgoing. She decided on a project that involved increasing the number of conversations she initiated. Just looking at the graph below motivated and

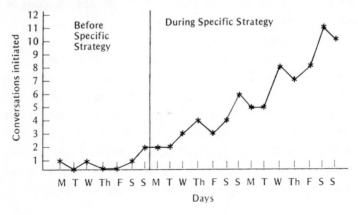

34

encouraged her to continue with the project because she could virtually see herself break out of it! (She used some strategies we will discuss in later chapters.)

The graph helps you see if any change has taken place. Notice that the solid vertical line on the graph divides the first week of recording from the second two weeks. This line indicates that during the first week of her project the woman only engaged in self-watching. She did not use any form of strategy to increase her conversations with people until the second week of the project. Her counted conversations to the right of the solid vertical line represent the two weeks during which this woman used some specific strategies designed to increase her chats with others.

What did this graph tell her? It told her that in this case self-watching alone was not as effective as self-watching *plus* some other form of strategy. When you plan your own self-change project, you will want to make this same sort of *before-after* comparison if you employ any of the strategies discussed throughout the rest of this book. *Remember:* if self-watching alone does not show any results on your graph during the first one or two weeks of your project, then use one or several of the strategies discussed in Chapters 4 through 11.

Most of the time you will want to use other strategies besides self-watching. However, sometimes watching alone will begin to change your behavior in positive directions. Sometimes you become discouraged because you think change has not occurred. But the graph may show you that a slight change has occurred. An elementary teacher wished to increase the positive remarks she made to her students during math class. Like the woman discussed on the previous page, the teacher used self-watching for a week and then employed some additional strategies during the following weeks. The graph below illustrates what happened to the teacher's positive remarks.

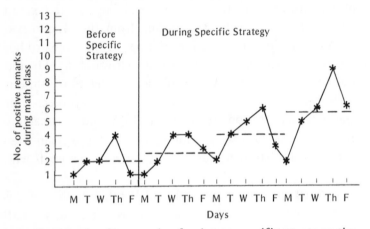

During the first week of using a specific strategy the teacher had great expectations. However, after comparing week one with week two, she became quite discouraged. Nevertheless, the dotted lines showing the average number of positive remarks made per day for each of these weeks revealed a slight change—from 2.0 to 2.8 positive remarks per day. This small change was enough to encourage the teacher to continue the project. During the third week of the project (the third week is to the right of the solid vertical line), the average had increased to 5.6 positive remarks per math class. *Remember:* Behavior that has taken some time to learn will not change overnight!

It was fortunate that this teacher used the graph and was thus encouraged to continue with her self-change program in very gradual steps. As a result she moved to an average of 11.7 positive remarks given during math class in three months. She noticed a significant improvement in her relationship with her students. They also progressed faster in their math lessons than they had in the past.

A Little Help from Your Friends

Some people who are self-watchers and self-changers find it helpful to share their charts and graphs with their family, friends, and lovers. This can often be a source of encouragement and motivation as well as joy, especially if you are making some progress. Some self-changers have taped their graphs on refrigerator doors, bedroom mirrors, or other highly visible places. You may want to do the same. But one word of caution: be sure that the people you share your project with will not ridicule you or put higher expectations on your project than is reasonable. In short, make sure that your friend or relative does not punish you when you don't measure up—or fail for a day.

Your Own Self-Change Project

In Chapter 2 you were asked to pinpoint what you wish to change. In this chapter you have been introduced to: (1) being a self-watcher and what it can do for you; (2) ways to count behavior, thoughts, and feelings (event watching, watching duration of an event, time-sampling); (3) apparatus for counting (pennies, notecards, and counters); and (4) record keeping (the chart and the graph).

What you need to decide now is how you will watch yourself. You also need to be aware that you will be making permanent records of your self-watching. If you wish to go ahead and watch yourself for a few days, go ahead. Remember that you will have to pinpoint, count, and record in order to make any sense of your observations. After a couple of days have passed, begin reading Chapter 4.

Part 2 *Strategies for self-change*

Up to this point I have taken you through several basic steps of self-change:

1. Motivation to change
2. Setting your own goals
3. Attaching numbers to your goals
4. Making mole hills out of mountains
5. How to be a self-watcher and why
6. Ways to count what you do
7. Record keeping

Having read Chapters 1 through 3, you now have the basics. If you elect to attempt a self-change project with these three chapters under your belt, you may do so. Some persons have made some rather significant turnabouts in their lives by using the seven basic steps above. However, others have not been able to change themselves through the use of these steps alone. Chapters 4 through 11 are designed to give some extra steps or strategies you can use to increase the effectiveness of steps 1 through 7. These chapters discuss techniques that other persons have used successfully. Some of these strategies will work well for you, others may not. The following chart will help you in selecting the chapters which may be useful.

Your Goal	Chapters (in order)
1. I want to overcome my fear of riding in a car (or any specific fear or anxiety).	7, 8, 4
2. I want to feel better about myself in general.	11, 8, 7, 10, 5
3. I want to become more motivated to change.	5, 6
4. I would like to become more straightforward or "up front" with people.	10, 7, 8, 11, 4
5. I would like to be able to say "no" to people more often.	10, 8, 7
6. I want to feel more relaxed in general.	7, 8
7. I need to make a stronger commitment to self-change.	6
8. I want to feel less guilty, depressed, hostile (any negative emotion).	8, 7
9. I want to become more responsible, *or* I want to stop procrastinating.	6, 5

Of course, many other goals might be listed on this chart. You may even wish to expand on it as you find various chapters useful for different goals you have set. Your expanded chart might be quite helpful to you as a ready reference guide to better mental health.

If you elect to try a self-change project without reading further chapters, *at least read* Chapter 9, "Is It Working?" after you are into your project for more than five days. It has additional suggestions for helping you to "regroup" if you're having difficulties.

What triggers you to act?   4

Do you remember Jim, the school teacher discussed in Chapter 3? He was concerned about his relationship with his four-year-old son, Cory. He watched his own behavior with Cory over a period of time and discovered several situations that seemed to lead him to make nasty comments to his son. Some of these events included: Cory spilling his ketchup or milk and cereal; Cory leaving his toys lying around the house; and Cory's delaying tactics when getting dressed for school in the morning. While Jim was watching himself make nasty comments, he also was noticing his surroundings. He was looking for the specific kinds of events or situations that seemed to trigger his angry outbursts. When Jim discovered those things that pushed him over the brink of anger, he was able to intervene by changing his *surroundings.*

Looking at your surroundings is a kind of necessary first step for dealing with any problem. A young woman, Mary, wanted to break a habit: chewing the inside of her mouth. Her habit gave her large sores on the inside of her mouth. She feared that this habit could cause a disease such as mouth cancer. She often had canker sores, and parts of her cheek lining were mutilated. While counting how often she bit the inside of her mouth, Mary also took note of the *times* during the day when she bit the most.

She discovered that her bicuspids palpitated most furiously in the morning just before and while she was driving to work. She noted that she chewed on the inside of her mouth on mornings when she was rushing to work. One event, then, that seemed to trigger Mary's chewing was getting up too late in the morning. She began setting her alarm clock ten minutes earlier each weekday morning, and during this period her biting decreased greatly.

How do you discover the events or surroundings that trigger you to act negatively? You discover them as you are self-watching. That is, at the same time you are watching how often you are doing or thinking something (watching events) or while you are watching how long something occurs (watching duration), you are also looking for events or surroundings that are present *just before* the negative action takes place. In Jim's case it was spilled food and toys lying around the house. For Mary it was getting up too late.

Janice, a college sophomore in one of my counseling groups, discovered that she was turning people off because her behavior was extremely aggressive. She decided to record two things. First, she wrote down each statement that seemed to turn other people off. Second, she wrote down what had happened *just before* the "aggressive comment." Since she could not write these statements down when she made them, she relied on her memory and recorded them as soon after as possible.

Here is a chart with Janice's "aggressive comments" and what happened just before each comment ("the trigger").

Aggressive Comment	The Trigger
1. Thursday while sitting in political science class, I told Mary she was "shallow as hell."	1. Mary said she thought Nixon was a good man.
2. Thursday p.m.: I told Chuck O. that he was a brilliant conversationalist (in a sarcastic tone).	2. Chuck had just asked me what I thought of the cold weather.
3. Friday p.m.: I told Pat that her party was absolutely bland.	3. Pat had just asked me if I was having fun.
4. Friday evening at Pat's party, I said, "Oh brother," rolled my eyes, and walked away from Jim W. right in the middle of a conversation.	4. He had just asked me to dance.
5. Saturday morning while playing tennis, I told Mary she serves like a jackass.	5. Mary had just double-faulted.
6. Saturday after tennis, I told an elderly man that if he didn't know where he was going he should not be driving the streets.	6. He had just asked us how to find an address I didn't know.
7. Saturday afternoon I said to Ann, "None of your damn business, Miss Prissy."	7. She had just asked me if I would be going to the homecoming dance with Chuck O.
8. Monday morning in Psychology 101, I told Dr.	8. Dr. Newberry had just said that behavior mod-

Newberry that he has some weird ideas about children. I also asked him if he's ever worked with children.

ification was a useful technique to employ with children.

From this chart and charts like it, Janice began to discover what triggered her to make aggressive responses. Janice found that any time someone stated something she disagreed with she would let that person have it. And if someone did or said something that made her feel uncomfortable or anxious, she would blast away. For aggressive comments 1 and 8 on Janice's chart, each of the triggers was a statement that Janice disagreed with. Most of the remainder of the "triggers" on the chart made Janice feel anxious or uncomfortable. For example, Janice was secretly afraid of expressing or receiving warm feelings from men. Thus, when Jim asked her to dance, she felt nervous, so she fled from the situation while managing to stay one up on Jim by putting him down and possibly causing *him* some anxiety.

Janice, then, began to watch for two types of situations or triggers. She watched for statements others made that she personally disagreed with, and she kept an eye open for situations that would make her feel threatened or nervous. Whenever she found herself in either of these types of predicaments, she would use a technique outlined by Dr. David Watson and Dr. Roland Tharp.*

Their technique is called "building in pauses." Janice decided that whenever someone began making statements

* D. L. Watson and R. G. Tharp, *Self-Directed Behavior* (Monterey, Calif.: Brooks/Cole Publishing Co., 1972), pp. 150, 158.

that she personally disagreed with, she would say to herself, "Now that is an example of the disagreement-with-my-personal-philosophy 'trigger' that usually leads to my turning the other person off. . . . I had better pause a moment." This pause allowed Janice some time to think of a more appropriate response. For example, instead of telling Mary that she was shallow as hell, Janice might have said, "No way do I feel that Nixon was a good man." In this way Janice at least would not be attacking Mary personally.

Janice used this same strategy for her second trigger—feeling threatened. Whenever she found herself becoming nervous or feeling threatened while around people, she would again "build in pauses." "Right now I am feeling threatened and if I don't watch it I'll end up blasting somebody and driving them away. . . . I'd better think of something else to say." Instead of calling Ann "Miss Prissy," Janice might have given Ann a simple yes or no answer.

Building in pauses allows time to pass. What you say to yourself during the pause becomes the *new trigger* for your next response. Thus you break up the automatic manner in which certain *old triggers* lead to negative responses. Building in pauses really replaces old, destructive triggers with new ones that are more constructive.

How do you record triggers? One way is to write them down in some detail, as Janice did. When you are first looking for the *kinds* of triggers that seem to produce negative behavior, writing the triggers *and* resulting behaviors down in detail helps you discover what *kinds* of triggers are creating negative behavior. Janice discovered two kinds of triggers that caused her negative reactions: (1)

people she disagreed with, and (2) statements or situations that caused her to feel threatened. When you are just starting to look for triggers, make detailed records, as Janice did.

Once you have found the kinds of triggers that are producing negative reactions, you can begin *coding* them with self-reactions that went with them. This method could be used for Janice's self-change program. If she figured out the kinds of triggers that were automatically leading to aggressive comments and wanted a quicker, easier way to record them, she could code the trigger "feeling threatened" with the letter T and code "disagreeing with statements" with the letter D. Whenever she found herself in a threatening situation she could record T on a notecard carried in her purse. Similarly, when she heard someone saying things she violently disagreed with, she could record a D as soon as possible. She could even code time of day by writing such things as "D—a.m." or "T—3 p.m."

If Janice's goal is to decrease the number of times these kinds of triggers result in aggressive comments, she also will have to code "aggressive comments." Every time she is faced with a T situation *and* follows with an aggressive comment, she should code "T—A" (A for aggressive). Each time she is in a T predicament and refrained from making an "aggressive comment," she should only record T. In this way she can tabulate her "batting average" at the end of each day through simple subtraction and division. Using the coding method will make recording easier and quicker. *Recording should be done as close in time to the original event as is possible.* This makes for more accurate and reliable records.

Watching what triggers your action is often a productive strategy for maximizing the chances for change to take place. Of course, it can only be productive to the extent that you can actually change your environment as a result of your observations. Jim, Mary, and Janice were all able to change old triggers into new triggers. These changes encouraged new behavior.

Let me briefly give a few more examples to illustrate the broad application of this strategy. Dr. Michael Mahoney and Dr. Carl Thoreson in their book *Self-Control: Power to the Person** suggest avoiding cigarette machines, buying only low-caloric snacks, and carrying only minimal amounts of money as effective ways of controlling smoking, overeating, and overspending. They also suggest some strategies for reducing the amount of food intake and dealing with that age-old "flab" dilemma.

How to Lose Weight
1. Eat in one specific room, preferably at one place in that room.
2. Avoid eating while watching television, talking on the phone, reading, or studying. This means that an ongoing activity like watching a football game must be interrupted while you eat, making eating less pleasant. (Who knows, while you're eating, you may miss Otis Armstrong's 98-yard punt return!)
3. Get in the habit of leaving small portions of food on your plate so that the "trigger" for meal termination is not a clean plate. Do not clean your child's plate, please!

* M. J. Mahoney and C. E. Thoreson, *Self-Control: Power to the Person* (Monterey, Calif.: Brooks/Cole Publishing Co., 1974), p. 25.

4. Arrange food portions so that they look larger by spreading them out over a plate or by using smaller dishes.
5. Eating slowly reduces the quantity of food consumed. Swallow one bite of food before putting the next bite on your fork.
6. Eat high-bulk, low-caloric foods (celery, carrot sticks) or drink large quantities of liquids before or during the meal to produce a sensation of "fullness."

Still other examples include arranging a study room so that all the cues lead to studying (a clean desk, pens, no *Playboy* centerfolds, etc.); putting up signs such as a "smiley face" to remind you to respond with praise to your children when they are playing cooperatively; a "Mr. Yeech" sticker on medicines to remind your two-year-old not to drink them; a "skull" ashtray to remind you not to smoke.

The list could go on endlessly. I think you have the idea. Rearranging your surroundings can help make a difference in the way you act.

Increasing motivation with payoffs

5

How Payoffs Almost Brought Full Stereo Sound to Tom and Trudee

My problem is that I bite my fingernails. I've been biting them for as long as I can remember. I have gotten them down so far that my fingers look hideous. I have tried, over the years, various methods to help me stop biting, but none has seemed to work. I have tried putting different solutions on my fingernails, but they tasted good, so that didn't help. I tried sitting on my hands when I felt the urge to chew; again to no avail. My willpower never seems strong enough to be of any help. I have become truly ashamed of my hands because of the looks of my fingernails. In fact, I really think it has affected my relationships with other people in a negative way. I do a good deal of entertaining in nightclubs and elsewhere. Because of my fingernails I've always been hesitant about expressing myself with my hands.

These were the opening comments of a young man, Tom, who wanted to try some of the strategies of self-change in order to overcome this habit. First he decided to count the number of times per day that he discovered himself with his hands in his mouth. His wife also counted and kept a tally whenever she was with him. They found

49

that just counting did not seem to make much difference: he was beginning to lose motivation to change.

Tom then decided to *increase his motivation through the use of payoffs.* With the cooperation of his wife, he tried a different approach.

Payoff Menu

1. Playing Pinball Machines. Since I had such a poor showing during my first several weeks, I decided that my first goal would be five occurrences of fingernail biting in one day. So, on any day that I reached five bites or less, I could allow myself the payoff of an orgy on pinball machines. This was quite effective since I'm a pinball machine fanatic.

2. Golfing with My Wife. Trudee and I agreed that on the first day that I got down to zero, she would go golfing with me.

3. Summer Sausage. One of my truly great fancies is my high regard for a particular brand of summer sausage that is sold at a local supermarket. If I could manage to obtain two straight days of zero, I would be able to eat as much of this kind of sausage as I pleased at the end of the second day.

4. New Tennis Balls. For three straight days of zero, I would purchase some new tennis balls, which I need badly. Otherwise I would have to play with the old balls.

5. Roberta Flack Recording. Since I admire the singing voice of Roberta Flack, my next goal would be four straight days of zero in order to get a tape recording of her songs.

6. Evening at Amusement Park plus Theater. By going for one straight week without biting my nails, Trudee and I

would spend an evening at an amusement park, including attending their theater.

7. Long-Range Goal. Trudee and I agreed that if I could keep from biting my fingernails less than five times during a six-week period (beginning July 3), I could purchase a long-desired stereo tapedeck and sound equipment to have built into our home.

Tom succeeded with the first six payoffs above but did not cash in on the stereo. It took too much time to get the payoff. The point, however, is that by building payoffs into his self-change program, he was able to move more closely toward his goal. And it may sound silly, but better looking fingernails gave Tom better and more comfortable relationships with people.

At this point you may be saying, "So what, I bite my fingernails, and it sure doesn't bother me. This guy must have had other deep-seated problems. What kind of a therapist are you, anyway?" Your question is understandable, yet there is another way of looking at the kind of problem Tom had. For example, some people don't mind wearing glasses, but others can't wait until they can afford to buy contact lenses. That doesn't mean that every nearsighted person who wears contacts has "deep-seated" problems, or should be in intensive therapy, or in an institution. It does mean that these people would rather not wear glasses. Tom would rather have fingernails than not. In either case many people simply want to change some aspect of their behavior. It is questionable—and possibly dangerous—to *assume* that a minor (though irritating) problem automatically means that a person has a deep-seated problem. The purpose of this book is to help you change what *you* want to change.

Let's examine Tom's program a bit more closely in order to make a few points about increasing motivation with payoffs. *First, it is absolutely critical that the payoffs you choose are very attractive to you.* Every one of Tom's seven payoffs were attractive to him. He enjoyed pinball machines, golf, tennis, Roberta Flack, amusement parks, theater, and stereo sound. This greatly increased the chances of the effectiveness of each payoff. You might have some difficulty thinking right now of several payoffs you could use to increase your own motivation. Here is a list of payoffs other people have used successfully; it may give you some ideas:

Eating fruit
Reading a novel
Playing volleyball
Camping
Drinking coffee
A day off work
Spending money
Making love
Going to the "spa"
Watching a football game on TV
Having a beer
Going out to eat
Taking bubble baths
Receiving a backrub
Smoking a cigarette
Playing catch with my son
Eating a piece of watermelon
Going to the beauty salon
An evening at the movies
Midnight snack

A half-hour of swimming
Buying some new clothes
Eating out for lunch
Calling a friend on the phone
A professional manicure
Leisure time to do whatever I want
Subscribing to a magazine
Playing bridge
Being alone
Cleaning lady once a month
Not having to clear the table

It may also be helpful to interview yourself again, as you did in the first chapter, but this time use a different set of questions. Watson and Tharp suggest some good questions to answer in finding payoffs for yourself:*

1. What kinds of things do you like to have?
2. What are your major interests?
3. What are your hobbies?
4. What people do you like to be with?
5. What do you like to do with those people?
6. What do you do for fun?
7. What do you do to relax?
8. What do you do to get away from it all?
9. What makes you feel good?
10. What would be a nice present to receive?
11. What would you buy if you had an extra five dollars? Ten dollars? Fifty dollars?
12. What behaviors do you perform every day?

* D. L. Watson and R. G. Tharp, *Self-Directed Behavior* (Monterey, Calif.: Brooks/Cole Publishing Co., 1972), p. 108.

13. What would you hate to lose?
14. What do you do with your free time?

From the list and this set of questions, you should be able to identify some potential and *attractive* payoffs.

What else should you know about payoffs? Any payoff you use should be accessible. What do you think of the following payoffs?

1. A trip to Hawaii
2. New ski boots
3. Making love
4. Quitting my job

If you're deathly afraid of airplanes, boats, and ski lifts, if your wife is at her mother's for a three-week visit, and if there are no other jobs in sight, your self-change program may be a bit of an uphill battle. Your payoffs cannot be very effective if they cannot be administered.

Finally, *the less time that elapses between your desirable behavior and the payoff, the more effective your payoff will be.* The only step in Tom's project that failed was the last one. He had to do something for six weeks before he could get his stereo. It was too long to wait, so it was not very effective.

Tom could have handled his last payoff in another way. He could have used what is called a "token" system in order to cut down the waiting time between the desirable behavior and payoff. He might have used poker chips or real money as tokens. If the full stereo system cost around $500 and the number of days in 6 weeks is 42, he might have put $12 away toward a stereo for every day he did not bite his nails. *Or* he could have put one blue chip and two white poker chips in a piggy bank or jar. It would take longer to earn the stereo system than the other pay-offs, but he would experience *part* of the full payoff each day he reached the goal. He still would have to do something for six weeks or more before he could get his stereo, but he would at least experience *part* of the final payoff every day that he did not bite his fingernails.

Poker chips, marks on a card or piece of paper, or actual money can be tokens. The point is they represent a partial payment toward the final payoff. And when the final payoff is in the somewhat distant future (this may mean only a week), "tokens" can help you feel the effects of the final payoff.

A word of caution: If you are using actual money for "tokens," be careful that you are not punishing yourself. For example, $12 per day may have been a financial burden on Tom and Trudee. If such was the case and they did use a money "token" system, they might want to use, for example, six months instead of six weeks as the waiting period. This would bring the daily payment down to a little over $2.

Leonard Makes Some Friends during His Free Time

The token system can work in many different kinds of situations. Leonard was referred to me by his fifth grade teacher when I was acting as a behavioral consultant for a suburban school system. Leonard was quite unpopular with his schoolmates and for good reason. He spent most of his time out of his desk distracting other children. Things had reached the point where Leonard would do anything to get a reaction—even a negative response—from his teacher or the children. When I asked him if he wanted friends, he began to cry. He said that no one liked him and that he hated school.

We talked about some things he might do in order to get people to like him more. Leonard came up with the idea of staying in his seat and getting his work done. So we planned the following strategy. Leonard announced to the class that he was going to try to stay in his seat more and not bother the rest of the class. This brought a resounding applause. I stated that this would be very difficult for Leonard, that he needed their help, and that he really wanted them to like him more.

We taped a notecard on Leonard's desk that looked something like this:

	Days				
	M	T	W	Th	F
1	✓	✓	✓	✓	✓
2	✓	✓	✓	✓	
3	✓	✓			
4	✓	✓			
5	✓				

Number of times out of seat during math class (row labels 1–5)

Leonard checked five times that he was out of his seat on Monday, four on Tuesday, two on Wednesday and Thursday, and only once on Friday. The class, teacher, Leonard, and I agreed that for each day that Leonard recorded fewer than five times out of his seat during math class (forty-five minutes of the day) he would earn five minutes of free time for the entire class on Friday afternoon. Thus during the first week of this token system, Leonard earned twenty minutes of free time for his classmates (five minutes each for Tuesday, Wednesday, Thursday, and Friday). Many of the children spent at least five minutes of their free time on Friday huddled around Leonard talking to him about his "project" and getting to know him better.

After the third week we all agreed on a new arrangement. Now Leonard would have to stay below four times out of his seat in order to earn the five minutes on any given day. Later the teacher and Leonard extended this to a minimum number *per day* as opposed to just during math class. It was exciting to watch Leonard become more popular with both his classmates and the teacher. His schoolwork had also improved considerably.

For Leonard we probably couldn't have picked a more attractive payoff than earning free time for the little people he desperately wanted to like him. Consequently Leonard worked very hard to stay in his seat, and after awhile it became almost second nature to him.

Now for some more words of caution about the use of payoffs. *Payoffs should very gradually be removed so that the mole hills you are trying to reach eventually become second nature or habits.* Not every teacher in Leonard's future is going to give the class free time if Leonard stays in his seat. If Leonard comes to expect this and he doesn't get it, he may be back where he started very quickly. So what is the solution? The teacher must gradually remove the free-time payoff, hoping that it will be replaced by the payoff of better grades, more favorable teacher response, and more friends.

What are the logistics of this: how is it done, practically speaking? One way would be for the teacher to negotiate with Leonard. Fewer and fewer minutes of free time would be given for each "good day." Thus after a couple of weeks, each successful day would only earn two minutes of free time, then one, and finally none. Another method might be to change payoffs. After a month or so, Leonard could deliver his own payoffs. For example, he could say positive things to himself on successful days: " I stayed in my seat during the whole math class today!" or "I'm having a good day." Hopefully Leonard's teacher would say similar things to him once in awhile.

A successful token system will begin with such things as points, check marks, or poker chips that can be cashed in for desirable payoffs. It will then move gradually away from external payoffs to more internal payoffs, such as, "Far out, I got a date with Nancy," or "I can't believe it. I'm starting to take some time just for myself; it feels super!"

Trouble-Shooting

If your payoff does not seem to be working, ask yourself two questions: (1) "Do I really think that I will stop doing that negative stuff (for example, biting nails or telling people off) or start doing that positive thing (for example, talking to more people, or talking more about my good points) just because of the payoff I have chosen? Is it attractive enough?"; (2) "Did I break my "mountain" down into small enough "mole hills" to maximize my chances to succeed?"

If the answer to the first question above is no, select another payoff, a more attractive one. Or if you have been cheating (giving yourself the payoff even though you aren't doing anything for it), get someone else to deliver the payoff, someone who agrees not to be a nag if you fail for a day or even a week. If you answer the second question in the negative, go back to Chapter 2 and read the section on "mole hills" and "mountains."

Finally, if motivation to change seems to be your biggest problem and nothing I've suggested in this chapter has increased that motivation, read Chapter 6. Try it. However, if that doesn't commit you to action, yet you still feel that change is necessary, see a professional therapist or counselor. Take the book with you and show it to her.

Self-contracting

6

That Was the Resolution That Was

"I am going to make a New Year's resolution to finish this book in 1975!" This was the verbal agreement I made with myself back in December of 1974. To my amazement, however, the entire month of January passed without one word being put on paper. Where had the time gone? "Oh well, eleven more months in 1975. I'll get started in February." Another week passed. Still no evidence of magic fingers on the typewriter. "Where did I put that Smith-Corona anyway? It was here in the study just before Christmas. Maybe I ought to read my first five chapters. Perhaps they could help me. Let's see mole hills, pin-point, record keeping, making the graph public, payoffs."

Contracting involves a written commitment, a specific statement of what you will do, how much and under what conditions. It usually should involve at least one other person. It takes private thoughts, such as, "I am going to finish this book in 1975," out of the secret domain and into the public eye. Instead of being a promise to do something, a contract is a statement of actions, steps, or mole hills.

The following self-contract moved me away from empty promises toward action.

Self-Contract

February 9, 1975
Date

Self: _Jerry Schmidt_

Other: _Karen Schmidt_

Goal: _To increase my book writing time_

Agreement

Self: _I agree to write on my self-change book for a minimum of eight hours each week. Any given writing interval must be at least two hours in length._

Others: _Karen Schmidt (my wife) agrees to read and comment on all written pages that occur during two-hour intervals, within the same day they are written._

Consequences

Arranged by Self:
(if contract is kept) _If I stick to the above agreement, at the end of each week (ending Friday at 5:00 P.M.) I will reward myself with an expensive cigar._

(if contract is broken) _If I do not keep the above agreement during a given week, I will do the yardwork by myself on Saturday._

Arranged by Others:
(if contract is kept) _Karen will (1) read and comment on all written pages finished during two-hour intervals; (2) type final copy each week I write for eight total hours; and (3) help me with the yardwork for one hour on Saturday during each week I keep the contract._

Signed _Jerry Schmidt_

February 29, 1975   _Karen Schmidt_
Review Date   Witness

There were two parties involved in this contract. I have made a written commitment to another person. It is not just another empty New Year's resolution in my head January 1 and gone January 2. The contract also contains goals with numbers attached to them. In order to receive my favorite cigar, help on the yardwork, and typing assistance, I must write for a minimum of *eight hours* during the week. Each time I write for a *two-hour* period, regardless of whether *eight hours* is reached for the week or not, I buy a book review and some comment time.

Payoffs chosen for this contract were very attractive to both Karen and me. She enjoys reading and making comments on what I write, and she also enjoys doing yardwork. At the same time it is highly satisfying for me to get immediate feedback on what I have written. It is assumed, of course, that for each week that I fail to keep the contract, Karen is authorized to refrain from yardwork and typing.

Rich and Lucille: The People Who *Always* Disagreed

Recently, a middle-aged couple came in to see me for marriage counseling. When I asked them why they had decided to begin therapy together, the wife, Lucille, stated that they had a communication problem and that both of them wished to change this. So the mountain for this couple was to "improve communication."

There was, of course, little we could do to "improve communication" until we started pinpointing and making mole hills out of a mountain. I asked Lucille and Rich to tell me what specific things, if changed, would bring about better communication. During the first session, we discovered two mole hills that could be developed into action programs for the next week. I wanted to be very careful to limit the goals and action programs to small manageable steps so that Rich and Lucille would not become overwhelmed or lost in their communication problems.

The first goal, or mole hill, was to decrease the number of times Lucille used the words *always* or *never* to refer to Rich's behavior. For example, if Rich failed to pick up his empty beer can and throw it in the garbage, Lucille would say something, such as, "you *never* throw anything away when it's empty. I *always* end up having to clean up after you!" This usually marked the beginning of an "unfair" marital battle in which a cross fire of destructive statements was aimed at each other's vulnerable spots. Since Lucille admitted that Rich often did discard rubbish and things he had used up, she agreed to allow him to count the number of times she said "always" and "never" in reference to his behavior during the next week.

The second mole hill agreed upon was to select three separate five- to ten-minute sessions per week (each on a different day) for positive feedback. During this time alone together, each partner was to tell the other things he/she appreciated about him/her. For example, if Rich had appreciated a warm, lingering kiss Lucille had given him the day before, this was the time to let her know how much he had enjoyed it. It made no difference whether or not he had expressed his appreciation when they kissed, he was to express his pleasure again during the positive feedback session.

In order to motivate this couple to fulfill their agreement and to insure that "communication" was clear, written contracts were developed. The first one is on the next page.

Self-Contract 1

<u>January 3, 1975</u>
Date

Self: <u>Lucille B.</u>

Other: <u>Rich B.</u>

Goal: <u>To decrease my "always" and "never" statements in reference to</u>
<u>Rich's behavior.</u>

Agreement

Self: <u>I agree to allow Rich to count and tally my "always" and "never"</u>
<u>referents to his behavior without arguing with him about it.</u>

Others: <u>Rich B. agrees to count and tally my "always" and "never"</u>
<u>statements without harassing me about such statements.</u>

Consequences

(If I break the contract)<u>If Rich thinks I am arguing about one of his</u>
<u>"tallies," Rich will say, "I will not argue," and leave the room.</u>

(If Rich breaks the contract) <u>If I think Rich is harassing me about an</u>
<u>"always" or "never" statement, he is to stop counting for the rest</u>
<u>of the week.</u>

Signed <u>Lucille B.</u>

<u>January 10, 1975</u>   <u>Rich B.</u>
Review Date   Witness

This self-contract differs somewhat from the one I developed for myself earlier in the chapter. Lucille's contract does not spell out any consequences for keeping the contract; it only defines the consequences if the contract is broken. Rich and Lucille felt that positive consequences or payoffs did not need to be written into the contract, since just being able to fulfill the contract would be a strong payoff. That's okay. Some persons feel that a self-contract is too restricting and mechanical if all consequences are specified. The real payoff came when by our next meeting Rich had not been able to count one "always" or "never." An entire week had passed without a destructive fight.

However, watch out for this "feeling too mechanical" idea. It can be merely an excuse not to work at changing yourself. The reason that making such a commitment as a self-contract may feel mechanical and awkward to you at first is that you have not defined your goals clearly enough in the past. Waiting until an action feels "natural" or completely "spontaneous" may be similar to expecting an *A* in calculus the night before the final exam although you haven't cracked a book all semester. Reaching goals and self-change are not easy. Ordinarily self-change is *not* spontaneous, and it does not feel natural. It is new, awkward, like a foreign language at first. *Self-change seldom occurs automatically.*

Questions
Up to this point I have discussed two contracts that turned out to be flaming successes. *What happens if you write up a beautiful contract but don't keep it? Then what?* If you fail to keep a self-contract, remember not to blame yourself and not to make excuses for yourself. Excuses and blame are two primary reasons for people failing to reach their goals. If you use excuses, such as, "I didn't have time to do it," or "It was his fault," you will miss another chance to become a better person. Self-blame certainly hasn't helped you change in the past. It won't help in the present, either.

But what can you do if you don't keep the contract? First, if you and the other party do not agree that all parts of the contract have been honored, you probably haven't defined those parts clearly enough. That is, you haven't pinpointed. Don't blame each other for not pinpointing. Merely plan together how you can make the contract more specific and clear. If necessary, get a third party to help you. In general, contracts that have numbers and consequences included in the agreements will have the best chance of being clearly understood by all parties involved. Thus, my self-contract in this chapter has a better chance of being clearly understood than the contract between Rich and Lucille. The phrases *without arguing* and *without harassing* in their contract are left to subjective human judgments. (Each partner was willing to let the other make these judgments. And so, in this case, further pinpointing was unnecessary.)

Second, you may have broken the contract because the task or behavior you agreed to was just too much to expect: the "mole hill" was too large. As mentioned in Chapter 2, there is nothing wrong with setting small, attainable, relatively easy goals for yourself and gradually increasing their difficulty.

Third, the payoffs or positive consequences for honoring the contract may not be desirable enough. Employ the strategies in Chapter 5 for "making payoffs attractive to you."

What if the "other" party in your contract begins to hassle you about honoring the contract? A young woman wished to decrease her use of the expression "you know" in regular conversations. She enlisted the help of her husband to count her "you knows" during certain times of the day when they were together. Not only did he count, but each time she uttered these unforgivable words, he would say something like, "There you go again, you muffed it." In short order this young woman had given up her project and was back to the "you know" syndrome.

Harassment from others, especially if they are close to us, usually does little to get rid of behavior. This woman solved the problem by getting her husband to contract that he would count her "you knows" without telling or hassling her about it. He agreed, and she was then able to continue with her project.

What happens if the other party doesn't agree to stop hassling you or agrees but still doesn't stop? If this happens, find a different party who will enter into such an agreement with you. If your self-contract is so personal that you do not wish anyone else to know about it, you can contract with yourself. Thus, the best contractual arrangement is with another person involved who will help motivate you, but if you wish to self-contract on your own, you may do so. The contract below is an example.

Decreasing Carbohydrate Intake Self-Contract

Behavior desired	*Payoff*
Three consecutive carbohydrate-free days	An evening at the movies
(following the first three days) A day of twenty grams of carbohydrates or less	A carbohydrate-free or carbohydrate-low midnight snack
Two consecutive days of the above	A half-hour to an hour of swimming at the pool in our building
For every consecutive five days of the above	Fun in the kitchen at a no carbohydrate cost factor: a Dr. Atkins recipe cooked, eaten, and enjoyed
For every five pounds of weight loss from the original starting weight (a graph was developed to record weight daily)	Purchase a new article of clothing *or* spend two nights at the movies

You might ask why this person used the movies for so many of his payoffs. He liked movies, that's why. And he knew that using movies as a payoff would increase his motivation to engage in desirable behavior. In this contract there is no one else involved to keep the person honest or encourage him to continue. If he spends a half-hour in the pool but consumes more than twenty grams of carbohydrates for two consecutive days, he has cheated on the contract. It is then more likely that he will continue to cheat if he does not make an attempt to find another party to help him administer the payoff. The person who wrote this particular contract, however, was quite successful. In addition to losing 22 pounds, he enjoyed innumerable midnight snacks, enjoyable swims, exciting movies, and several articles of stylish clothing. He was able also to convince his wife to go on the same diet with a similar payoff schedule.

At least one more important point needs to be made with regard to this young man's "self-administered" contract. He used food as a payoff for decreasing food intake. That is, he employed a different form of the undesirable behavior to serve as a payoff. That was a very smart thing to do. He was overweight at least in part because food was already a powerful payoff for him. So, he used nonfattening foods to serve as a payoff for cutting down on fattening foods (high-carbohydrate foods). Some persons have smoked a good-tasting *cigar* while driving home in the evening because they had *cut back* on the number of cigarettes smoked at work. One school teacher allowed herself a "guilt-free" cigarette on the evening of each day that she cut back her normal cigarette intake by *two.* In this way she was able to decrease her average cigarette consumption from about a pack (twenty) to about five per day.

Your Self-Contract

Now that you have seen how others have developed self-contracts, write one of your own. Remember that it is preferable to write it with another party involved, but that it is possible to create a completely "self-administered" contract. You may want to tally the number of days that you keep the contract on a separate sheet of paper as an extra incentive. Making your contract and tally sheet public by posting it on the refrigerator door or elsewhere may be still another worthwhile incentive to consider. You may have to alter your contract several times before it really says what you want to accomplish. That is fine. Perhaps the single most important thing to consider in composing a contract is to attach numbers to your goals. It is also usually worthwhile to build in consequences or payoffs. Go ahead now. Develop those empty New Year's resolutions into real commitments.

Relaxing yourself 7

Our society encourages us to be tense and anxious. Everyday pressures push on us from all directions. "I must get that report done." "When will I ever get to finishing that basement?" "I've got three couples coming for dinner in two hours, and I'm not half ready for them yet." "If there were only more hours in the day." "Sometimes my head feels like it's going to explode, and when I feel like that I'm a real pain for everybody around me." "My butterflies get so bad sometimes that I can hardly function." "Whenever I get ready to take a test or make a speech, I get so nervous that I can't think straight and I forget what I'm going to write or say."

These are just a few of the statements people have made to themselves or others because of stress and anxiety. High stress usually keeps us from functioning as we would like. It certainly prevents us from performing as well as we are capable.

Why Should You Be Relaxed?
There is research evidence to support the belief that we all need to experience a certain amount of arousal or anxiety in order to be motivated to do much of anything. The purpose of this chapter is not to suggest that you should not experience anxiety. We experience anxiety every day.

However, if anxiety is experienced at such high levels that it interferes with our important life goals, it needs to be dealt with.

You are at a party where most of the people are, at best, only acquaintances. You had mixed feelings about going in the first place, but here you are! Perhaps you'll find a new friend. As usual, small talk between you and one other person comes relatively easy for you. But now there is a group gathering, and you begin to look somewhat frantically for the punch bowl. You begin to feel those familiar signs of nervousness. Your heart seems to be pounding faster; you want to impress someone, but you're not sure you can. You begin to wonder if you have anything interesting to say. Someone may become bored with you. You find yourself clamming up, perhaps dreadfully holding on to a cocktail in the hope that someone will seek you out for conversation. You end up leaving the party early, and when you get home, you feel like a dismal failure.

Chances are you have been victimized by your own anxiety. You were not able even to talk about things you know a good deal about, especially when four or five people were listening. Since you have assumed that parties are only for interesting conversationalists, your anxiety prevented you from saying some things that just might have appealed to others. In short, your inability to relax to any degree prevented you from enjoying yourself.

If you could have somehow controlled your anxiety or caused yourself to relax, chances are two things would have happened. One, you probably would have been less hesitant to speak up when that group began to gather around you. You would have been less concerned about whether what you were saying was "fascinating" or not. Two, you probably could have more easily accepted the fact that you are not a brilliant conversationalist and thus allowed yourself to have a good time anyway. Anxiety tends to put pressure on us to perform when it is not necessary to perform.

When Does Relaxing Yourself Help You?

You can relax under a variety of stressful circumstances. The following list suggests some of these life situations:

> Headaches, migraine
> Nervous stomach, ulcers
> Shyness caused by nervousness
> Shortness of breath caused by anxiety
> Perspiration
> Accelerated heartbeat
> Giving a speech
> Taking a test
> Talking with someone you are afraid of
> Flying in an airplane
> Talking with someone important
> Making a complaint
> Saying "no" or letting people know where you stand
> Feeling anxious about sexual intercourse
> Paying someone a compliment
> Asking someone for a date

Physical conditions, such as ulcers, hypertension, and migraine headaches, should be attended to by a medical doctor. Do not rely upon relaxation to "cure" such physical conditions. However, relaxation *along with* medical treatment can be instrumental in recovering from some of these ailments.

Do not expect relaxation to help motivate you or to make you want to do something. It is not a motivational technique. Relaxation is designed to help you cope with anxiety and tension. It is intended to decrease tension that keeps you from acting the way you would like or leads you to feel poorly about yourself.

How to Relax

Several psychologists have written about methods for relaxation. Some are based on muscle relaxation techniques; others rely on visual imagery; still others are based on "talking yourself" into relaxation.

The purpose of *muscle relaxation* is to experience the difference between *tension* and *relaxation* in your muscles. This is done through a series of exercises designed to help you experience this difference.

Sit or lie in as comfortable position as you can. Make sure that your legs and arms are uncrossed. Remove or loosen any article of clothing that causes you even a slight amount of discomfort. If you wear contacts, it would be best to remove them. It also would be best to do these exercises alone unless others in the room are serious about learning how to relax and will do the exercises with you. While you are in this comfortable position, read the following relaxation instructions without doing them.

Clench both fists tightly, as if you were squeezing all the juice out of an imaginary orange in each hand. Notice the muscles in your fingers and lower forearm . . . they are tight . . . tense . . . pulling. Clench your fists like this for about five seconds . . . then relax . . . just let your fists go . . . drop the imaginary orange in each hand. Pay attention to the sensations you now have in the muscles of your fingers, hands, and fore-arms as they relax. There is a sort of flow of relaxa-tion—perhaps a kind of warmth—in those muscles. Notice and enjoy this relaxation for about twenty to thirty seconds. Okay, clench your fists again, tightly. Notice the tension, especially from your fingers, and lower forearm. Now relax . . . let go. . . just allow the muscles to loosen. The relaxation is not something you make happen, but something you allow to happen. Notice the difference between *tension* and *relaxation* in those muscles.

Repeat this procedure a third time.

Now reach out in front of you with both arms . . . stretch forward with your arms . . . like a lazy Tom cat. Move your extended arms over your head . . . reach for the sky . . . hold it. Now stretch your arms out to the sides, back to the overhead position, again out in front of you, and let your arms drop to your lap. Allow the arms to relax. Again feel the release of tension, this time in the muscles of your upper arms, shoulders, and upper back. Enjoy the lack of tension in these muscles as they become more relaxed . . . still more relaxed . . . more relaxed than ever before.

Repeat this procedure again until your upper arms, shoulders, and extreme upper back are completely relaxed. This usually takes from two to four times, as do most muscle relaxation exercises.

Add the other muscle relaxation exercises one at a time. The list below tells you which muscles to tighten and relax for each exercise. Remember that each time you do an exercise you should tense the muscle for about five seconds and then let go completely with that muscle group, experiencing the contrasting relaxation for twenty to thirty seconds. Repeat each exercise three times during each relaxation session. (A relaxation session will last about twenty minutes.) In order to obtain maximum results you should spend at least one session per day relaxing. The more practice you get in muscle relaxation the easier it will become to control your anxiety in everyday life. The suggested muscle groups that need to be relaxed during each session are listed below. Don't do any exercises yet. Just read the list and become familiar with it.

Muscle Relaxation Exercises

Muscle Area	Instructions	Tension Location
Hands	Clench and relax both fists.	The back of your hands and your wrists.
Upper arms	Bend your elbows and fingers of both hands to your shoulders and tense the bicep muscles. Relax.	The bicep muscles.
Lower arms	Hold both arms straight out and stretch. Relax.	The upper portion of the forearms.
Forehead	Wrinkle your forehead and raise your eyebrows. Relax.	The entire forehead area.
Forehead	Frown and lower your eyebrows. Relax.	The lower part of the forehead, especially in the region between the eyes.
Eyes	Close your eyes tightly. Relax.	The eyelids.
Jaws	Clench your jaws and relax.	The jaws and cheeks.

Tongue	Bring your tongue upward and press it against the roof of your mouth. Feel tension, then relax.	The area in and around the tongue.
Mouth	Press your lips tightly together. Feel tension, then relax.	The region around the mouth.
Neck	Press your head backward. Roll to right, shift roll to left, and straighten. Relax.	The muscles in the back of the neck and at the base of the scalp, right and left sides of neck.
Neck and Jaws	Bend your head forward, press the chin against the chest. Straighten and relax.	The muscles in the front of the neck and around the jaws.
Shoulders	Bring your shoulders upward toward your ears, shrug, and move around. Relax.	The muscles of the shoulders and the lower part of the neck.
Chest	Take a deep breath and hold it for five seconds. Relax.	The entire chest area.
Abdomen	Tighten your stomach muscles and make your abdomen muscles hard. Relax.	The entire abdominal region.
Back	Arch your back from chair. Relax.	Lower back.
Thighs	Press your heels down as hard as you can, then flex your thighs. Relax.	The muscles in the lower part of the thighs.
Legs	Hold both legs out and point your toes away from your face. Relax.	The muscles of the calf.

Legs	Hold both legs out and point your toes toward your head. Relax.	The muscles below the kneecap.
	Relaxed state—easy breathing.	
	Arise, refreshed.	

When you are familiar with the muscle groups you will need to relax and the method of tensing and relaxing muscles, you will be ready to go ahead and try a relaxation session. There are several ways to do this. Since you should not read this book while you are doing the exercises, you may want to stop now and memorize them. Some people have recorded the instructions on audio tape and then played them back while relaxing. Remember the following *critical points:*

1. Allow at least five seconds for tensing the muscle.
2. Allow twenty to thirty seconds for the relaxation phase.
3. Do the exercises in a place where you won't be interrupted for twenty to thirty minutes.
4. Repeat each exercise three times in a row before proceeding to the next muscle group.
5. For maximum results practice relaxation at least once per day.

Go ahead now. Relax. Get rid of some tension and allow your body to become recharged. Think of your relaxation period as your time for yourself. Close your eyes and relax. Enjoy it!

What Will Muscle Relaxation Exercises Do for You?
After you have exercised for one session per day for a week, you will begin to notice that you can "get into" the

relaxation more rapidly and that sometimes you won't need the exercises per se in order to relax a particular muscle. When this begins to happen, drop the exercise for that muscle and merely tell that muscle to relax. Again, it's not something you force or make happen. You just say to yourself, "I'm going to let my chest muscles relax . . . they are loosening just like the strings on a guitar . . . I'll allow them to loosen . . . I'm enjoying the lack of tension." Once you are able to do this with a few muscle groups, begin to practice it in real-life situations.

You could have used relaxation at the party that was mentioned earlier in this chapter. Several people begin to gather around, and the topic of conversation is something you are familiar with. You are beginning to think of things you would like to say. You get "butterflies" and hesitate. But now before the butterflies can get the best of you, your relaxation exercises come in handy. You say to yourself, "I'll let my stomach muscles relax . . . they're loosening. . . ." Now you have a better chance of responding. Instead of fully concentrating on your nervous stomach and negative thoughts about your "stupid ideas on the subject," you now let go. You use muscle relaxation to allow yourself to relax, to allow tension to be released instead of held in.

When tension is held in too long and with too much intensity, it takes up too much concentration and energy. We are then unable to function well. We have used up too much energy for controlling anxiety and thus have little left over for responding favorably to our surroundings.

You can use these exercises in a number of ways. They may help you fall asleep at night. If you suffer from ulcers or migraine, use them along with your medication.

These exercises come in handy just before you are going to give a speech. Try them while flying in an airplane. Actually, anytime that you have physical signs of anxiety ("butterflies," sweaty palms, ice cold hands, rapid heart rate, or a feeling of dread), you can use these relaxation exercises to calm yourself down.

Anyone who has anxiety management problems should know these exercises. You have a better chance of performing at your best capabilities and feeling good about yourself if you are relatively relaxed as opposed to being highly anxious.

Problems with the Exercises
Some of the exercises may give you cramps if you hold the tension too long or tense the muscles too hard. If that occurs, decrease the five-second tensing interval, and don't tense so hard. You could also find an alternate way to tense the muscle that is becoming cramped. (Be careful when you use the neck rolling exercise. Do it gently and slowly.)

If you are having trouble getting a muscle to relax, try taking a deep breath while tensing and letting it go while you relax the muscle. If that still doesn't do the trick, move on to the other muscles and come back to the troublesome one later.

If you notice a muscle twitching during your exercises, don't be alarmed. That merely means that your body in general is relaxing.

Finally, if you have followed all of my suggestions and are still having difficulty with relaxation, consult a psychologist who has training in behavior therapy and systematic desensitization. You might also want to purchase *Progressive Relaxation Training* by Dr. Douglas Bernstein and Thomas Borkovec, an excellent book on relaxation.*

Talking Yourself into Relaxation

A second form of relaxation training stems directly from the exercises you have just learned. Once you are relaxed by the exercises, use words to encourage and expand your looseness and lack of tension. Each time you exhale, for example, you say a soothing word to yourself, such as, "calm," "heavily relaxed," "control," "easy," or "quiet." If you do this often enough during your relaxation sessions, it will begin to carry over into real-life situations. For example, when you are experiencing anxiety and there is no time to go through a series of muscle exercises, you might begin to breathe deeply and repeat silently, "calm," each time you exhale. No one will know what you are doing except you, and you may be better able to handle the situation. You might even use a few inconspicuous exercises just to get started. You can clench your fists and let go, tighten your stomach and let go, and do the tongue exercise on the roof of your mouth. Then begin to use the calming words.

Actually, if you take more of these tension-reducing steps in real life, chances are life will become easier and the tension reduction itself will become easier and quicker. Remember, Rome wasn't built in a day, and *you* can't be *rebuilt* in a day. That's why you should not give up easily. It will take time and practice to become more at ease with yourself and others. But these techniques do work. Research shows that relaxation training is more effective for

* D. A. Bernstein and T. D. Borkovec, *Progressive Relaxation Training* (Champaign, Ill.: Research Press, 1973).

anxiety than any other psychotherapeutic strategy. The next chapter will discuss some rather new tactics that also hold high promise for tension reduction.

Other Strategies for Dealing with Anxiety

Perhaps some other ways of helping yourself relax have occurred to you. Here are some extras that you might use either by themselves or in combination:

1. Just before doing something that causes you tension, take a deep breath and let it out rapidly.
2. Tense one or two muscle groups that are unnoticed by others and let go.
3. Focus for a few seconds on something very pleasant (a relaxing scene or some pleasant event that is coming up in the near future).
4. Smile.
5. Stretch.
6. Say something to yourself, such as, "All I need to do is take my time," or "It's actually amusing how anxious I'm making myself become over nothing."

Several points deserve repeating. One, don't expect to become Mr./Ms. Cool after a day of relaxation. It probably would be a good idea to do the muscle relaxation exercises for about a week before even attempting to use relaxation in real life. Two, try various techniques and combinations of the tactics mentioned in this chapter for coping with everyday anxiety. Three, don't just try something once; try it *at least* on ten to fifteen occasions before giving up. These strategies have worked before for many people. Four, the next chapter has more suggestions for anxiety management. Read it. Five, have fun with relaxation. Don't make it a chore. Enjoy it.

Talking to yourself 8

For years all of us have been under the impression that talking to yourself was, at best, a sign of peculiarity. Certainly some of the oddest folks in my home town were the ones who wandered about carrying on conversations with themselves.

Why am I asking you to "talk to yourself?" You've heard of the "practice of medicine." When I was a boy, the family doctor told us to drink as much milk as possible. Now I'm only to drink milk on my cereal in the morning because drinking more may be hazardous to my health. We have moved back and forth along many extremes in psychology as well. We call this the "practice of psychology." However, in the past we have not checked out very carefully which methods work best.

Recently psychologists have been doing a good deal of research on the effectiveness of various techniques. "Talking to yourself," or thought control, has emerged as one of the most promising of these techniques.

Talking to Yourself
A middle-aged businessman came to me to discuss his marital problems. In the course of therapy he told me that one of his basic worries was money. He said that for years he had kept track of every penny he and his wife spent. He

itemized and counted very carefully how much each of them spent. At the end of the week whoever had spent the most money was the "culprit," the villain. This led to fierce marital battles over money. It was not long before this man and his wife were hiding what they spent, especially on themselves. This also led to vengeful spending sprees by the wife and a "separate business expense account" for the husband. Most of their conversations in the evening centered around shrewd interrogations about "what did you spend money on today?"

I told the husband to try a simple technique called *screaming internally*. Each time he began to worry about what his wife had spent, he was to scream internally (silently), "Get out!" five times in succession. This got rid of the continuous, nagging thought that his wife was spending money. Every time that he began to worry about his wife's expenditures, he was again to scream internally, "Get out!" five times in succession *or* until the negative thought about his wife left him. This strategy usually takes a good deal of time and hard work to succeed, but this fellow got rid of "money-obsessed" thoughts within a few days by using the screaming internally tactic.

A secondary effect came a week later, when he ceased to itemize all expenditures. He did, however, continue to balance the checkbook and itemize tax-deductible expenses. His relationship with his wife also began to improve. The less he thought about his wife's spending habits, the less he interrogated her in the evening. The more he was able to back off and trust her with money, the less she seemed to be spending.

Screaming internally takes on the same general format as other thought-control techniques:

1. *A negative* thought triggers you to do something undesirable to you and others. (For example, "I'm no good because I didn't get an *A*, or "Strong people don't ask for help.")

2. A *positive* thought triggers you to do desirable things for yourself and others. (For example, "I didn't get straight *A*'s in school, but that doesn't make me an inferior person," or "John F. Kennedy was certainly a strong person, yet he was continually asking for help from members of his cabinet.")

3. Once you have identified the negative or positive thought that is triggering certain behavior (for example, the businessman above identified, "I'm scared to death that Ruth is spending too much money," or "I'd better call her to check if she's home instead of out shopping"), then you decide what to do with the thought.

4. If the thought is *negative* and you wish to *decrease* its frequency, you can use one or a combination of the following techniques:

   Screaming internally

   Countering

   Internal self-punishment

   External self-punishment

5. If the thought is *positive* and you wish to *increase* its frequency, you may use internal self-payoff as a strategy.

In general, then, thought control takes this form: a *negative or positive thought* followed by *a thought-control technique which is designed either to decrease or to increase the frequency of the original thought.*

Decreasing Negative Thoughts

There are four procedures that may be used to decrease negative thoughts: screaming internally, countering, internal self-punishment, and external self-punishment. I have already introduced screaming internally. Let me discuss it in a bit more detail.

Screaming internally. Our businessman was able to rid himself of self-destructive thoughts by stamping out these thoughts. The label *screaming internally* suggests two things. One, "screaming" suggests shouting or crying out loudly. When you use this technique, shriek the "get out" with extreme intensity and anger. But do it silently. Some persons have actually shouted this phrase out loud while driving down the highway or in the privacy of their own homes. That is okay too, but the advantage of screaming internally is that you can do it in public without attracting attention.

Other phrases may be used to scream at negative thoughts:

Get out of here.
Get away from me.
Quit bugging me.
What a stupid thought.
Go to hell.

The important thing to remember about this method is that you have to keep doing it over and over again before it really takes hold. Do not give up too quickly. It takes time and persistence, but it will very likely work if you keep at it. Each time you get that negative thought, repeat whatever phrase you use until the self-destructive thought does not return. It probably will take fifty to a hundred screams before you notice positive results.

Countering. At this point you may be wondering what kind of negative thoughts you are having and how to identify them. Here are some self-destructive thoughts that other people have had:

I should be happy all the time.

Healthy people don't get anxious or upset.

I have to make other people like me at all times.

Every problem has a perfect solution.

Making mistakes is awful and proves that I am not a worthy person.

Because of my terrible upbringing I can never change or amount to much of anything.

Strong people don't ask for help.

I should never be openly proud of myself.

I must never show anyone my weaknesses.

I am inferior.

In order to decide anything I must be 100 percent sure of my decision.

There is a hidden part of me that mysteriously causes me to do things I don't want to do.

Other people should always trust me.

People shouldn't act the way they do.

These thoughts often trigger us to behave in less than desirable ways.

Although this list is not exhaustive, it does describe some of the self-thoughts that keep us from being the people we want to be. *Countering* is the second procedure for decreasing these negative thoughts. It is really a statement that argues with the negative thought.

Let's return once again to the money-minded businessman. His negative self-thought was, "I'm scared to death Ruth is spending too much money." At that point he could *counter* with, "Every time I start worrying about Ruth spending money, I get our relationship into trouble." Or he could counter with, "I've got other more important things to think about besides whether Ruth is shopping or not."

You could also use countering in an anxiety-arousing situation, such as the party described in Chapter 7—"Relaxing Yourself." A group of people gathers around you. You feel very nervous about what you will say. You have taken a deep breath, relaxed a few muscles, and used words like "calm" and "confident" to allow yourself to relax. Yet you still feel like leaving so that you won't have to expose your "stupidity and shyness" to the others. If you are feeling stupid and inept in that situation, chances are you are saying some negative things to yourself. You might be saying, "I have to make other people like me at all times," or "If I talk about something, it must be interesting or fascinating."

Find a sheet of paper and list as many counters as you can for these two negative self-thoughts. Let your imagination run wild. Do this for about five minutes.

Some possible counters for these negative self-thoughts that others have come up with are listed below. Some of them will be similar to yours. Others will not. Compare them with yours. They may give you some new ideas.

Negative Self-Thought No. 1:
"I have to make other people like me at all times."
Counters:
1. "There's no way that I can make other people like me twenty-four hours of the day."

2. "Shirley tried to please everyone, and she had a nervous breakdown."
3. "Not even Jesus Christ pleased everyone."
4. "Other people are too unpredictable to please 100 percent of the time.
5. "I'll wear myself out trying to please everybody."
6. "I've got to please myself, too."
7. "When I try to please everyone, I end up being 'wishy-washy'."
8. "I haven't got time to please everybody."
9. "Sometimes other people have to please themselves."

Negative Self-Thought No. 2:
"If I talk about something, it must be interesting or fascinating."

Counters:
1. "Who says so?"
2. "Very few things that people say are fascinating."
3. "I've not met one person in my life who was fascinating or even interesting all of the time."
4. "Not even great orators fascinate me or hold my interest throughout a speech."
5. "I'm expecting myself to be God incarnate!"
6. "I'm being too hard on myself."
7. "That's a stupid thought! It just makes me more nervous."

Here are a few more situations with their accompanying negative self-thoughts and resulting self-defeating feelings and behaviors. A few counters for each negative thought are included. You add a couple more just for practice.

Situation:

Jeff couldn't start his car, so he was late for work.

Negative Thought:

"Good employees aren't late for work. Everyone is disappointed and angry with me because I'm late."

Resulting Feeling:

Guilt, inferiority.

Resulting Behavior:

Avoided people all day. Snapped at customers. Did not explain to boss why he was late.

Counters:

1. "Everyone else in the office comes in late now and then."
2. "Tough—it couldn't be helped."
3. "That's silly! Every good employee in history has been late at least once!"

4. _____
   _____
   _____
5. _____
   _____
   _____

Situation:

Alverta's classmates criticized her written report.

Negative Thought:

"My report must not be any good. I'm a lousy writer. I shouldn't be in school. I think I'll quit."

Resulting Feeling:

Inferiority, disappointment.

Resulting Behavior:

Alverta tore up her report and decided to quit school.

Counters:

1. "It's not unusual for the students to criticize written reports in this class. That's one of the purposes of the course."
2. "All of the other reports were criticized also."
3. "Mr. Haber told me I am a good writer."

4. _____

_____

_____

5. _____

_____

_____

Situation:

Alan Tentative was turned down for a date by Sally Upstart.

Negative Thought:

"Women must think I'm undesirable."

Resulting Feeling:

Inferiority, depression, embarrassment.

Resulting Behavior:

Alan never called Sally again. In fact, he didn't call another girl for one month.

Counters:

1. "I had a date with Sharon last week. She must think I'm desirable."
2. "What a silly conclusion to come to. I was only turned down for this one date! That doesn't mean that women in general find me undesirable."

3. "What I'm really saying to myself is that I should feel inferior and depressed because Sally turned me down for one date. That's nonsense!"

4. _____

_____

_____

5. _____

_____

_____

What's your "situation"? Most of us have one or two kinds of situations that we usually don't handle very well. Think of one, and try to identify what negative feelings you get in that situation. Write down the *situation* and *resulting feeling* that you often get. Follow the pattern outlined in the examples above. Next, write down the *negative thought* or thoughts that seem to be triggering negative feelings and self-defeating behaviors. Finally, develop some *counters* that you can use to oppose the negative thoughts.

Once you have done this you are ready to use countering in this sequence. You are in your situation or imagining yourself in that situation. The negative thought occurs. Then very aggressively you tell yourself all the effective counters that you have developed. You don't let up. You repeat the most effective ones over and over until the counters win the argument over the negative thoughts.

You can combine *screaming internally* and *countering*. First say, "get out," or, "stop," whenever the negative thought slips into your head. Then continue your onslaught against the negative thought by countering.

Internal self-punishment. Still another strategy that you can either use by itself or in combination with the first two is internal self-punishment.

Get yourself in a relaxed position (in an easy chair, etc.). Allow yourself to relax for a few moments by using a few of the suggestions for relaxing discussed in Chapter 7. Now imagine yourself in your situation. Make the situation as "real" as possible. "See" the colors and shapes; "hear" the sounds; notice details in your imagined scene. Now go ahead and say the negative thoughts that you get in that scene or situation. Say these thoughts several times. Stop. Next comes the internal self-punishment. Imagine all the horrible things that could happen in your life if you continue with these negative thoughts. Let your imagination run wild. What are the most undesirable consequences of these self-defeating thoughts. How will they utterly destroy your life? Work hard and aggressively on this for about a minute. Repeat this at least three to five times at each sitting.

For example, think of the negative consequences of the thought, "If I talk about something, it must be interesting or fascinating." What are some horrible things that could happen to someone's life if they continued to use this negative thought? Here is what one young woman used for internal self-punishment:

If I continue to think this way, I'll end up seldom speaking to anyone for fear that it won't be interesting enough. If I don't speak to other people, I'll have few friends. Maybe I'll end up with no friends. If I get that lonely, I'll become very depressed. I'll end up in self-pity, and I'll drive others away, even though I don't want to. I may even consider suicide. What if I ended up an alcoholic? Maybe I'll get so depressed that I'll have to be hospitalized.

The intended effect here is to punish the negative thought so much that it will occur less and less frequently. Research shows this procedure to hold real promise for behavior change, especially if it is used in combination with payoffs for effective use of counters. I will discuss this in greater detail in the section on increasing positive thoughts in this chapter.

External self-punishment. This technique is rather simple yet often quite effective. Whenever a negative self-thought comes to mind, snap yourself with a rubber band that you have previously placed around your wrist. This, again, has the effect of punishing the negative thought and often decreases its frequency.

Increasing Positive Thoughts

It is not enough merely to decrease negative thoughts about yourself. You must also increase positive self-thoughts. Research in psychology strongly supports this idea. There are at least two ways to do this: internal self-payoff and external self-payoff.

Internal self-payoff. Dr. Rian McMullin and Mr. Bill Casey have written an excellent book called *Talk Sense To Yourself.** They suggest several tactics for dealing with negative thoughts and increasing positive ones. One of these strategies is called SP/SR (self-punishment/self-

* Rian McMullin and Bill Casey, *Talk Sense to Yourself* (Lakewood, Colorado: Jefferson County Mental Health Center, 1975), pp. 43-44.

reward). It increases the effectiveness of the internal self-punishment procedure in several ways:

1. First go through the internal self-punishment exercise described earlier in this chapter.
2. When you have thought of all the worst possible consequences of your negative thought, you can stop.
3. Now, again think of your situation. Be sure to imagine it in great detail. However, this time imagine yourself making positive self-statements. Use some of your counters. Just think rational, constructive thoughts that will most likely lead to desirable actions on your part. Imagine handling the situation very well, feeling good, acting calmly and intelligently. Do this for about a minute; then stop.
4. Immediately start imagining the best possible consequences of your positive self-thoughts. Use your imagination and feel free to exaggerate. For example, "If I can realize that problems do not have perfect solutions, then I'll be a much more effective boss. I'll get a raise!" Keep on doing this. When you have thought about all of the positive outcomes that could develop from your positive thoughts, you can stop.

You should repeat this entire sequence three times at each sitting.

I have included an example of SP/SR for a person working on depression:

1. She imagines the situation: "I call my husband at work. He's not in. He went to lunch. The secretary doesn't know where. It's early (about 11:30 a.m.). I say to myself, 'He's probably out with a woman,' or, 'Why isn't he available when I need him? He should

be there when I'm blue. This is terrible. I must have someone to talk to, I must talk to my husband, NOW.' I start crying."

2. "If I truly believe that things must always go my way and that it's terrible if they don't, then these things can happen to me: I'll start to act like a small child, crying whenever things go wrong or I don't get my way. I'll end up pushing him toward someone else. Other people will begin to see me as unstable and unable to cope with even small things. I'll let small petty things upset me to the point where they ruin my entire day, week, my entire outlook on life! I won't have any happy days, because I'm bound to be let down every day!"

3. "I call my husband at work. He's not in. He went to lunch. The secretary doesn't know where. It's early (about 11:30 a.m.). I say to myself, 'Good for him. He's been working through the lunch hour all week. He deserves a nice long lunch. But I still need someone to talk to. I'll call Gale and ask her if she wants to go to lunch at Valentino's.' I call Gale and arrange to have lunch with her at 12:30."

Another form of internal self-payoff can be used very simply. Whenever you handle a situation well, no matter what the technique, say something positive to yourself: "That was pretty neat, Joel!" or "That's super! I did it! I finished this chapter!"

Summary
These techniques have one basic purpose: to help you make changes that *you* want. You, your needs, and your personality will determine what works best in a specific situation.

Is it working?

9

Let's take time for a breather. I've been throwing a lot of different strategies your way. I hope you are not confused or running the various tactics together in your mind. A review might help keep things in perspective.

In Chapter 1, I gave you a brief description of this book and asked you to interview yourself. Then in Chapter 2, I asked you to pinpoint some personal goals for yourself. After pinpointing, you were taught to be a "self-watcher." In Chapter 3, I emphasized that just watching yourself often changes your actions. I also stated that if watching yourself alone doesn't change things for you, you should try some of the techniques found in Part 2 of this book. I even included a guide in the introduction to Part 2 that suggests which chapters would be helpful for particular problems you might be facing.

Then I discussed several strategies that you can use to encourage self-change:

1. Changing your surroundings—Chapter 4
2. Increasing motivation through payoffs—Chapter 5
3. Self-contracting—Chapter 6
4. Relaxing yourself—Chapter 7
5. Talking to yourself—Chapter 8

There are two more basic intervention techniques that I will discuss in Chapters 10 and 11. The point I wish to make here is that *no matter what technique or combination of techniques you use, you still must go back to the graph to decide whether you are changing or not.*

For example, when you completed the self-interview exercise in Chapter 1, you may have discovered that you very much would like to enter one of three vocational fields: law, teaching, or the ministry. You realize that these fields require good verbal and persuasive skills. At present you feel that you have fewer verbal skills than, perhaps, even the average person. At this point some guidance counselors would give you ability, aptitude, and interest tests and tell you to steer clear of any careers that would demand your giving speeches, etc. This theory of guidance I call the "best fit theory." That is, you should accept whatever some test or expert tells you. You should then try to find a station in life that "best fits" your psychological profile, as described by that test or expert. If I had continued to live my life by the best fit theory, I would not be nearly as pleased with my life as I am today. I certainly would not be writing this book!

The philosophy of this book goes beyond the best fit theory: while you should always consider intelligent advice, you, not the "experts," should be the final judge of what you are "best fit" to be. Assume that you decide to stick to your goal: you plan to become an attorney, teacher, or minister. You have decided to try the step-by-step process for self-change suggested in this book. First, you pinpoint several mole hills that will lead you in the direction of your three mountains:

1. Over a month's period I will increase by four the

number of conversations that I initiate each day. That is, no matter what strategies I use to increase initiated conversations, by the end of the month I will be averaging four more initiated conversations per day than at the beginning.

2. During the next six months I will take one speech class at the university.

3. I will express a personal opinion in at least two conversations per day for the next week. During the following week, I will increase "personal opinion statements" by one per day.

4. Each time I am in a group of two people or more, I will ask at least one question of the person I feel closest to in the group.

Next, you decide on an ingenious method of counting. At the beginning of every day you place pennies, nickels, and dimes (ten of each) in your right pocket. Every time you initiate a conversation (speak first) with someone, you move one penny from your right pocket to your left; nickels are for counting "personal opinion statements"; dimes count questions asked in a group. At the end of the day you can sort out how well you are doing on mole hills one, three, and four by simply counting the pennies, nickels, and dimes in your left pocket. (By the way, if you need to spend some of your pocket change during the day, be sure to spend it out of your right pocket.)

Initially you are determined to change by simply counting—no "fancy gimmicks" like relaxing yourself or talking to yourself. However, after a week you discover (through counting and graphing—discussed in Chapter 3) that you are not reaching the goals you have set. Reluctantly, you reread Chapters 4 through 8. You decide that relaxing yourself and talking to yourself might not be such bad ideas after all. The graph on the next page draws a good picture of what happened.

Notice that in this case self-watching alone did not seem to increase the number of initiated conversations. However, when you added relaxing and talking to yourself, you hit four on three separate days.

That's the beauty of going back to the graph! It can tell you so many things about what is effective for you and what seemingly is not. Notice also that personal opinion statements were occurring only once a day at the most while self-watching alone was employed. Again, however, the two added strategies of relaxing and talking brought the daily average to over two personal opinion statements per day. Finally, although you were reaching your goal of one question asked in a group per day when you used only self-watching, the addition of the two extra strategies increased this number dramatically.

In this way you check out whether particular tactics are useful or not for reaching certain goals you've set for yourself. In a sense you are doing psychological research when you graph the results of your self-change strategies.

Graph the results of your labors, and remember, the only way you can count anything that can be represented on a graph is to break your goals down into mole hills with numbers attached to them. You *cannot count,* "I will improve my verbal skills," or, "I will improve my ability to give speeches." You *can count* the number of "personal opinions expressed per day."

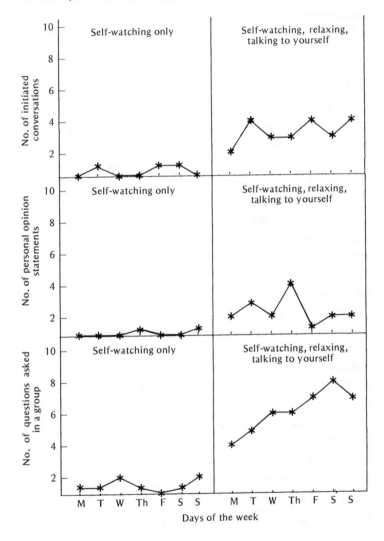

A Record of Initiated Conversations,
Personal Opinion Statements, and Questions Asked in a Group

If It's Working, When Will You Stop?

You must decide when you have changed enough in the right direction to stop using your formal counting and graphing procedures. You may never want to stop. Or you may want to check yourself now and then, counting for one day each week or month just to make certain that your self-change is permanent. I believe that it's important to make these little future checks. It's gratifying to know that you are still moving in the right direction. It also can be useful information to know that things have gone downhill and that you again need to use some kind of self-change scheme.

There is a second kind of decision that you will have to make. When will you stop using the intervention technique or techniques that you started with in order to bring about self-change? If you intend to remove a particular strategy, remove it gradually. If you are using payoffs such as tokens or points that you can later "cash in," you could require more and more points for the actual payoffs you are earning. You also could make yourself eligible for payoffs only on certain days, decreasing the number of days eligible by one day each week until you are no longer using them. If you do this, you may want to substitute internal self-payoffs ("I did it! That's super! I just keep improving") for the external payoffs used in your point system.

Many of these strategies are used on a continuing basis by increasing numbers of people. You also may find yourself consistently using several of these strategies.

If It's Not Working, What Went Wrong?

If your chart shows your self-change program is a real flop, resist the temptation to give up. Try one or all three of the following.

1. Develop smaller mole hills. Attach smaller numbers to them. (Instead of having to initiate a conversation four times per day, set a goal of only having to initiate three times per day.)
2. If you're using payoffs, make them stronger and more frequent.
3. Throw in another self-change strategy. Two strategies are sometimes better than one.

Summary

A few chapters ago I warned against assuming that people's problems are "deep-seated" and complicated. This same advice applies to using the methods in this book. Start simple. If you need a really complicated system of counting or recording or payoffs, you will find out soon enough—and be able to add what you need. By starting with a simple program, you will be able to build the specific kind of program you need and get a clear idea of what works—and what doesn't.

Getting what you need

10

One of the most helpful things anyone ever said to me was spoken by a former supervisor of mine: "You don't need a license to practice who you are," he stated flatly. I doubt that I'll ever forget the impact that statement has had on my life over the past five or six years.

You don't need a license. Or do you? Ever been in this scene? You're sitting in a classroom. Two or three persons near you light up a cigarette, cigar, or pipe. Smoke really bothers you. In fact it often gives you headaches. But you don't dare say anything for fear that you will upset someone. But who is most upset *now?*

Here's another scene. You are waiting for a friend. She's already fifteen minutes late. Your stomach starts to rumble. You toss an antacid mint into your mouth. Oh that damned ulcer! There she is . . . finally, only twenty minutes late this time. You can't remember when Dorothy was on time. You really want to say something to her about it, but you don't want to hurt her feelings or make her angry. In the meantime your stomach feels like it's going to turn inside out; you're boiling inside and *you* are the one with hurt feelings.

Let's try one more. Jim and Judy Boring called to invite you to their place for a very quiet evening, too quiet! It's not that you don't like them. They just aren't your type. You went over to their place a month ago, not because you really wanted to, but because you didn't want to let them down. You even invited them over for dinner a couple of weeks ago. Why?! Because you can't say no. So now, instead of enjoying your Friday evening, you'll grin and bear it. Correction, you'll grin and migraine it!

It's not enough that I've told you to talk to yourself in Chapter 8. Now I'm hinting that you should be rude to people by telling them what you feel. Yes, I am telling you to tell people what you feel. No, I'm not telling you to be rude to people. You might even ask which is more rude—to go on giving the Borings the impression that you want to be close friends or to start saying no to their invitations?

In the smoking scene an assertive response would have been, "When I smell a lot of smoke I get terrible headaches and can't concentrate on what's going on in class." An alternative response might have been, "I'd rather you didn't smoke. It gives me a headache." If stated in a matter-of-fact tone, such responses often bring the desired result. And you are more apt to get your needs met—less apt in this case to get a headache.

What about Dorothy? What can you say to her? You might say something like, "When you are late for an appointment we've made, my ulcer acts up and I really get upset." My guess is that you'd be surprised at the positive response forthcoming from Dorothy.

Aggressive, Nonassertive, Assertive

When you are angry, disappointed, or frustrated, you can respond in at least three different ways. You can retaliate with an *aggressive response* ("Get to the back of the line buddy before I bust you in the chops"). You can disregard your own feelings and needs by giving a *nonassertive response* ("Oh well, one more person in front of me in line won't hurt . . . I guess?!"). Or you can offer an *assertive response* that expresses your feelings and needs openly ("Sir, I've been waiting in line for a long time now and I have another appointment soon, would you mind stepping to the end of the line?"). This last response is straightforward. It is said in a flat neutral tone, almost the way a computer would say it. It has the effect of letting the other person know what your needs are without putting him on the defense as the aggressive response would.

Thus, an aggressive response shows disregard and disrespect for the other person. It has the effect of stomping on others and putting them on the defensive. When those around you are continually on the defensive, chances are, in the end, you won't get what you need. And even when you do get your needs met by using an aggressive response, it usually shows disregard for the other person. This doesn't mean that you shouldn't get angry or that you must never shout at anyone. There are times when you have little choice but to respond aggressively. However, assertive behavior is more humane and effective.

A nonassertive response covers up your strong feelings: no one else knows what you are really thinking or feeling. When you give a nonassertive response, the other person assumes that you feel fine about the situation, even though you are suffering inside. You re~~'~~ can't blame others for responding in selfish ways to don't tell them what you need. It's simil said, "I want my husband to be more a not about to tell him . . . . If he car certainly not going to tell him!" This "Read my mind. It's a real challenge.'

that few people claim to be mind readers these days, so the challenge becomes insurmountable!

An assertive response states directly and clearly what you need. Assertive people tend to look you in the eye, move their bodies freely, share their feelings with you, receive compliments easily, occasionally talk about themselves, and sometimes openly disagree with you. It's about time that we acknowledge the right to have an ego. No, I didn't say "ego trip"; I said ego.

There are a few more things to keep in mind about assertive behavior. One, when you wish to make an assertive statement, look the other person straight in the eye. Two, sit up or stand up straight. Do not slouch. Three, say your words slowly and distinctly. Do not slur or mumble your words and do not hang your head while you are speaking. Four, feel free to use your hands to help express what you are saying. This makes you appear more concerned and interested about what you are expressing. The result of all this is to convince the other person to notice what you are saying and to take you seriously.

You might practice making assertive statements into a mirror. Look straight into the mirror. Don't slouch. Use your hands to help express yourself. Speak clearly, loudly, and slowly. Say a few things you would have liked to have said to someone in the past few days. Do not make an aggressive response or a nonassertive statement. Speak in a straightforward, matter-of-fact manner (don't attack the other person).

If you feel that your main difficulty is the way you ' the words, practice making assertive responses into a ʳecorder. The clearer and more distinct your words ' e better. Have a friend or spouse judge how you are doing by listening with you to the tape. Then go ahead and record a second time while looking into the mirror and practicing your eye contact. Sit up straight and use your hands and body to highlight what you are saying. Listen again.

Still another technique is to role-play assertive comments with a partner. A close friend might be willing to try this with you.

Finally, when you are constructing assertive responses, it might be helpful to think of them in this form: "When (the event that's bothering you) I feel (the feeling that you are experiencing) and I (can't, have trouble, am unable to) (the consequence of the event for you)." Remember the assertive response given in the smoking scene? "When I *smell a lot of smoke* (the event) I *get terrible headaches* (the feeling) and I can't *concentrate on what's going on in class* (the consequence)." Here's another example. "When you fight like that in the living room, I'm scared to death that you will break something valuable."

Assertive responses do not have to follow this form in order to be effective. But chances are that if you include the ingredients of these examples (the troublesome event for you, your feelings about it, the consequences for you), you'll have a good chance of putting your message across.

Practicing Assertive Responses

Now I'll present some situations in which you might want to make assertive responses. I'll describe the scene briefly, give an aggressive and a nonassertive response, and ask you to write an assertive comment in the blank space. Then I'll give a few assertive responses so that you can compare them with your written assertive statements.

Situation:

You have just been served a rare steak at a restaurant, but you ordered it medium.

Aggressive Response (to the waiter):

"What a lousy joint. At these prices you'd think a person would get some decent food" (leaving a penny tip to accent your point).

Nonassertive Response:

You eat only half the steak. When the waiter asks you if everything is okay, you smile and say, "Uhm, on yes, fine" (while your stomach growls for more food).

Assertive Response:

_____

_____

_____

Suggested Assertive Responses:

"Waiter, I ordered this steak medium and it's much too rare. Would you please return it?"

"I ordered mine medium and as you can see it's been cooked rare. I do not want any pink showing."

Situation:

A salesman has just gone through considerable trouble to show you some merchandise you prefer not to buy. You feel a bit guilty about just giving him a flat no.

Aggressive Response (you decide to argue with him):

"I saw the same product at Lear's for two dollars less. Besides you're just like all other salespeople—trying to con me with a cheap product." *Note:* It is usually not a good idea to argue with a salesperson over a product you don't want. He'll usually win the argument.

Nonassertive Response:

"Well I suppose it's a good product. You've certainly done a good job explaining it. I just don't know if I can . . . uhm . . . afford it . . . or . . . uh . . . if I *really* need it . . . but . . . uh." SOLD!

Assertive Response:

_____

_____

_____

Suggested Assertive Responses:

"That's a very thorough presentation, but I'm not interested in buying any of your merchandise."

"It sounds as though you have some good products there, and when I'm ready to buy, I'll let you know."

"I certainly appreciate all your trouble, and I'll give it some thought . . . . Thank you . . . have a nice day" (as you walk swiftly out of the store).

"No, I do not want to buy anything." (How's that for being straightforward??)

Note: The first three responses above will help alleviate your guilt because you've recognized the "trouble" the salesperson has gone through.

Situation:

Someone has just given you a compliment about the clothes you are wearing.

Aggressive Response:

"Yes, when I buy clothes I buy quality stuff. At our house we don't go for the bargains you do. But that's just a matter of what you want."

Nonassertive Response:

"Oh, it's not much. Really not too stylish. You know . . . when you're poor like we are. . . ."

Assertive Response:

Suggested Assertive Responses:

"Thank you. I like brightly colored clothes."

"Thank you. I'm glad you like it."

Situation:

One of your children has just done something that made you a very proud parent.

Aggressive Response:

"Holly, you did a nice job this afternoon, but you still need to work on . . . and your timing was off when you got to. . . ."

Nonassertive Response:

(You don't say anything because you're too lazy or you figure she'll just get a big head . . . or perhaps you'll embarrass her or yourself.)

Assertive Response:

Suggested Assertive Responses:

"You did a super job this afternoon, Holly! I'm really proud of you."

"It's great to have a daughter like you. You made my day."

Here's a list of other situations in which people have had problems asserting themselves. Pick out a few that give you trouble. Write out some assertive responses for each and practice saying or doing them. Remember the old rule about breaking mountains down into mole hills. That is, start your own assertive responses in situations that seem the easiest and work up to the harder ones.

Starting conversations with acquaintances or strangers
Making or accepting dates
Returning merchandise
Asking questions for fear of sounding stupid
When someone pushes in front of you in line
Telling someone you no longer wish to date them
Asking your roommate to do his fair share of the cleaning
Reminding someone of the money he owes you
Asking a friend to do a favor for you
Expressing your own opinions about things
Expressing love and affection toward people you care about
Making complaints
Giving and receiving compliments
Refusing requests, especially if they are unreasonable
When someone interrupts you in the middle of a conversation

Notice that in the list above as well as in the exercises you have done that the idea of "assertive behavior" has been expanded beyond merely making complaints and responding out of frustration. Assertive responses can be used in a wide variety of situations. The purpose of making the assertive response is to clear up communication so that both you and others know where you stand. It is important that persons around you know when you need something that you don't presently have (like privacy, more change back from a cashier, replacement of guaranteed merchandise, or more love-making from your spouse). It is equally important that they know when you are feeling warm and affectionate toward them. Suffice it to say that most persons are tuned into *their own* needs. And the easiest way you can get others to notice what *you* desire is *to state your needs directly and flatly.*

Your Own Assertiveness

A worthwhile project might involve counting the number of assertive responses you make during this next week. Then, the following week try to increase this number by three, four, or five. Graph the results each week for several months. Use relax yourself and talk to yourself strategies to help you. For example, take a deep breath, let it out, and say to yourself, "I have a right to ask for what I need," or "How can Linda know that I feel good about what she did, unless I tell her?"

Finally, if you want more information about assertiveness, read *Don't Say Yes When You Want To Say No* by Herbert Fensterheim and Jean Baer.*

---

* H. Fensterheim and J. Baer, *Don't Say Yes When You Want To Say No* (New York: Dell Publishing Co., 1975).

How do you feel about yourself?

For the most part, this little book was written to help you feel better about yourself. It is based upon what I feel are some basic facts:

1. A self-directed person, like you, often learns best when *action*, as opposed to talk, is the basis for learning.
2. Your present situation can be improved without rehashing your negative past.
3. The opportunity to develop and plan *your own* self-change increases the chances that you will in fact grow and develop.
4. You can learn how to change and feel better about yourself by observing others who have changed.
5. Attitudes and feelings about yourself are altered primarily by trying out new actions in real-life situations.

The fact that you have read this book says that you want to act on rather than merely talk about your problems. Not that such things as "talking things out" with a friend or in psychotherapy are meaningless exercises. Nothing could be further from the truth. However, there comes a time when you must decide to change or not to change. If you decide not to change, that's fine, of course. Accepting yourself as a person is extremely important. However, if you wish to change, action is the key.

And your past is a significant part of you. Yet, dwelling on your mistakes of the past does little to help you change in the present. Self-blame, if continually practiced, can only drag you down.

No one can force you to change. You must decide that for yourself. There is some psychological research which suggests that self-directed change is the most permanent. Again, this is not to say that a psychotherapist or a friend cannot be helpful in the process, but self-improvement basically is up to you, even in psychotherapy. I've given you several self-change strategies in this book, but you must decide whether you'll use them or not.

I have told you about many persons who have used the techniques described in this book. There is, perhaps, no better way to learn than to read about and observe what others do that has been successful and model after them. Try that. When you see someone who is doing the kinds of things you would like to do, get to know that person. Observe what kinds of things that person is doing that produce "success." Go as far as you can to break this successful behavior into mole hills. Then practice it.

Strengths Building

I have suggested a number of methods for self-change and increasing your self-concept. Here are a few additional exercises thrown in for fun. Try a few. They are specifically designed to help you identify and build on your own strengths.

    1. Create a "strengths collage." Gather up old magazines and find pictures, words, phrases, etc. in them that

help describe your strengths, your skills, and your strong points. Cut out the pictures or portions of pictures and phrases that describe the strengths you have, and paste them on a piece of newsprint or cardboard in any pattern you choose. Have fun with this. If you are a member of a family, do this as a group project. Create your strengths collages individually and then post them. You may want to share the meaning of your posters with each other. This may lead to some pretty neat "strokes" for everyone.

2. Each day, list on paper the successful experiences you've had and think about why they were successful. Again, consider the skills you brought to those successful experiences. These achievements do not have to be earth shaking. For example, perhaps you got a bargain on a fishing pole, or maybe you called a friend and arranged for a weekend outing.

3. Each month, select a person you admire (a fictional character in a novel, an actual historical or contemporary figure, or a person you know). Observe, talk to, or read about this person. Compile a list of strengths that this person actively used or presently uses. Compare the strengths of this person with your own. Then pick one strength you would like to develop and break this mountain down into mole hills.

4. List your success experiences for the past year. It may help to think of one success for each of the past twelve months or one for each of the past four seasons of the year. Once you have made this list, analyze each of the successes for what personal strengths you have that contributed to that success.

Don't cop out by saying, "I was just lucky," or "I had nothing to do with it." Chances are that any achievement of yours is at least in part attributable to your own skills. Identify them.

5. Relax yourself by using the exercises discussed in Chapter 7. Once you feel that lack of tension, begin to imagine yourself in one of the successful scenes you've identified above. Enjoy the scene to the fullest. Say things to yourself like, "I really did that well," or, "That felt super," or, "I feel good about that." Allow yourself a couple "success scenes" at each sitting. Spend about two or three minutes on each episode.

Summary

The self-change strategies presented in this book have been shown by psychological research to be effective with varying kinds of human problems. I invite you to try them out. I'd like to give you a few afterthoughts to consider and reconsider as you use these techniques:

1. Try each strategy you select several times. Do not give up on a particular technique because it has failed twice in a row. Try again. It has taken you a lifetime to learn undesirable habits. It will take some time and practice to *un*learn them.

2. You can certainly use this book in conjunction with psychotherapy or counseling. If you do wish to be in counseling while you try out some of these tactics, be sure your counselor knows about these particular psychological principles.

3. Make postchecks on your behavior after your self-change program has been discontinued. That is, if you have stopped using a technique like "talking to your-